WHY VIDEO GAMES ARE GOOD FOR YOUR SOUL

PLEASURE AND LEARNING

James Paul Gee

WHY VIDEO GAMES ARE GOOD FOR YOUR SOUL

PLEASURE AND LEARNING

James Paul Gee

COMMON
GROUND

This book is published at theLearner.com
a series imprint of the UniversityPress.com

First published in Australia in 2005
by Common Ground Publishing Pty Ltd
www.theLearner.com

National Library of Australia Cataloguing-in-Publication data:

Gee, James Paul.
Why video games are good for your soul: pleasure and learning.

ISBN 1 86335 574 X (pbk).
ISBN 1 86335 575 8 (PDF).

1. Video games - Psychological aspects.
2. Computer games - Psychological aspects. 3. Video games and children.
4. Video games and teenagers. 5. Learning, Psychology of. I. Title.

794.8019

Cover designed by Darling Deer Design.
Typeset in Australia by Common Ground Publishing.
Printed in Australia on 80gsm Offset.

Contents

CHAPTER ONE

INTRODUCTION

Good video games are good for your soul. Now there's a statement that begs for some qualifications!

First, what's a video game? What I mean are the sorts of commercial games people play on computers and game platforms like the *Playstation 2*, the *GameCube*, the *Xbox*, and the handheld *Game Boy*. I mean action, adventure, shooter, strategy, sports, and role-playing games. I mean games like *Castlevania, Half-Life, Deus Ex, Metal Gear Solid, Max Payne, Return to Castle Wolfenstein, Tony Hawk Underground, Rise of Nations, Civilization, Age of Mythology, The Elder Scrolls III: Morrowind, Allied Assault, Call of Duty, Tales of Symphonia, ICO, Pikmin, Zelda: The Wind Waker*, and *Ninja Gaiden* to name some random good games off the top of my head. There are many others.

Second, what does "good for you" mean? Next to nothing is good or bad for you in and of itself and all by itself. It all depends on how it is used and the context in which it is used. Is television good or bad for children? Neither and both. It's good if people around them are getting them to think and talk about what they are watching, bad when they sit there alone watching passively being baby-sat by the tube (Greenfield 1984). The same is true of books. Reading reflectively, asking yourself questions, and engaging in a dialogue with others, is good for your head. Believing everything you read uncritically is bad for you and for the rest of us, as well, since you may well become a danger to the world.

So good video games are good for your soul when you play them with thought, reflection, and engagement with the world around you. They are good if, as a player, you begin to think and act like a game designer while you play the game, something good games encourage. After all, players co-author games by playing them, since if the player doesn't interact with the game and make choices about what will happen, nothing will happen. Each page of a book and each scene in a move is predetermined before you see it and is the same for every reader. Many acts and their order in a video game, however, are open to player choice and different for different players.

So, then, what's a good, as opposed to a bad, video game? It would take a book longer than this one to explicate what makes good games good and gamers don't know how to put it all into words. You have to play the games. Good games are the ones gamers come to see as "gaming goodness", "fair", and sometimes even "deep"—all terms of gaming art. Good games are the games that lots of gamers come to agree are good, though they rarely think any one game is perfect.

Some games, like *ICO* or *American McGee's Alice*, get discovered late and become underground classics, while others, like *Half-Life* or *Zelda: The Wind Waker*, nearly everyone agrees from the outset are good. Then there are games like *Anachronox*, which didn't sell well and received some rather tepid reviews, but is, I'm telling you, a darn good game—you see I have my own opinions about these matters. In fact, different gamers like and dislike different games and different types of games.

OK, then, what for heaven's sake is your soul? And what could playing video games have to do with it? Once, years ago, I had the special experience of going back into time and living for several years in the Middle Ages. The details need not detain us—you'll just have to trust me on this—but, believe me, that experience taught me what souls meant in one context. That is not what I mean here.

Too often in the world today people from all sorts of religions believe that those who don't share their beliefs will go to some sort of hell and, worse, they are sometimes willing to make life hell for others here and now to help them, whether they like it or not, avoid going to hell. Or, perhaps, they just make life hell for others to ensure that they themselves will go to heaven, having displayed their merit by removing a suitable number of infidels. While I do retain a certain nostalgia for the Middle Ages, that nostalgia plays no role in this book.

So what could I mean by "soul?" I mean what the poet Emily Dickinson meant (Dickinson 1924):

> My life closed twice before its close --
> It yet remains to see
> If Immortality unveil
> A third event to me
>
> So huge, so hopeless to conceive
> As these that twice befell.
> Parting is all we know of heaven,
> And all we need of hell.

What Emily Dickinson is talking about here is not the immortality, heaven, and hell of traditional religion (Dickinson was skeptical of traditional religion at a time and place where that was socially dangerous, especially for women). She is talking about a fact that every human being knows and feels, a fact that defines what it means to be human. This fact is that we each have two parts. One of these parts is our body. If you truly traumatize the body, it will die and it can die but once, which is, indeed, a mercy.

But there is another part of us, a part to which different religions and cultures through the ages have given different names. This part—let's just say it is our "soul"—can be traumatized over and over again and not die, just as in the case of the two emotionally damaging events to which Emily Dickinson alludes. No mercy here, as we all very well know, unless you have been very fortunate, indeed, in your life. The rest of us have, if old enough, already died more than once. This part—this soul—is immortal in the sense that, until the body goes, it can go on suffering grievously over and over again, suffering many deaths, unlike the body which can die but once.

But it is because we have this soul part that events and other people can take on such a charge for human beings. It is because we have this soul part that events and other people can give us what we know of heaven here on earth. It is only because losing a loved one, either by death or parting, as Dickinson is alluding to, can give rise to such pain that loving others can rise to such joy. You can't really have the one without the other. Having the charge, the spark, is heaven and losing it is hell. But you can't have it if there is no chance of losing it, that's the way of life for us humans. That's why we "need" hell. There is no heaven without hell, no positive charges without risk of negative ones.

Emily Dickinson very well knew, then, that it matters hugely whether life here and now for people is heaven or hell. It matters hugely whether we help make life heaven or hell for others, whether we murder or rejoice their other parts, their souls, that part of them that cannot die as long as they have their bodies. It matters. We can be complicit with murder without having killed anyone. The world can murder us several times over long before it takes our bodies.

The Middle Ages saw to it that peasants and the poor died many times before they died. The rich got off more easily, though, by the nature of life itself, they, too, paid their soul dues. Modern life offers more opportunities, but more complexity, as well. For many people—perhaps, all of us at times—modern life offers too much risk and too much complexity (Kelly 1994). We don't really understand what's going on around us, lots of it just doesn't make any good sense, at least as far as we can tell. We can understand why some people turn to fundamentalism to garner secure "truths" without thought and reflection. It is, indeed, an attempt to save their souls, to protect themselves from the traumas of modern life, a life where often the rich get richer, the poor get poorer, and everyone suffers risks created by other people, even people clear across the globe.

If people are to nurture their souls, they need to feel a sense of control, meaningfulness, even expertise in the face of risk and complexity. They want and need to feel like heroes in their own life stories and to feel that their stories make sense. They need to feel that they matter and that they have mattered in other people's stories. If the body feeds on food, the soul feeds on agency and meaningfulness. I will argue that good video games are, in this sense, food for the soul, particularly appropriate food in modern times. Of course, the hope is that this food will empower the soul to find agency and meaning in other aspects of life.

This book is primarily about the pleasures—the charge—that good video games can give people. These pleasures are connected to control, agency, and meaningfulness. But it is also about how good games create deep learning, learning that is better than what we often see today in our schools. Pleasure and learning: For most people these two don't seem to go together. But that is a mistruth we have picked up at school, where we have been taught that pleasure is fun and learning is work, and, thus, that work is not fun (Gee 2004). But, in fact, good videos games are hard work and deep fun. So is good learning in other contexts.

Pleasure is the basis of learning for humans and learning is, like sex and eating, deeply pleasurable for human beings. Learning is a basic drive for humans. School has taught people to fear and avoid learning as anorexics fear and avoid food, it has turned some people into mental anorexics. Some of these same people learn deeply in and through games, though they say they are playing, not learning. The other people who often say they are playing when they're working hard at learning are those professionals—scientists, scholars, and craftsmen—who love their work. There is a reason for this kinship between gamers and professionals and that will be one of the things I deal with in this book.

This book is written for anyone interested in video games, whether this be gamers, people interested in learning, or people interested in the pervasive role video games play in modern society and across the world. After all, games are a massive economic force today and an even more major cultural force, since they are a shared culture among many young people across the globe (Kent 2001; King 2002; King & Borland 2003; Poole 2002). This book is meant to be a contribution to the emerging field of game studies, though I argue that game studies should interest a wide array of people, gamers and non-gamers alike (Aarseth 1997; Juul 2004; Laurel 1993; Murray 1998; Salin & Zimmerman 2003; Wardrip-Fruin & Harrigan 2004; Wolf 2002, 2003).

I have a confession to make, though. I offer here a partial "theory of games". I hate to tell you this, because I know lots of you will not like to hear it, since "theory" sounds so boring. But I hasten to add, the book contains precious little jargon (much less than readers had to endure in my earlier book *What Video Games Have to Teach Us About Learning and Literacy*, 2003). I hasten to add, as well, that I never venture too far from talking about actual games. Things stick pretty close to the ground, I hope. No arcane philosophy, I promise (well, maybe you found the stuff on the soul arcane).

Well, we have to deal with it. We all know the topic is looming over us. What about violence and video games? Does playing video games lead people to be more violent? More ink has been devoted to this topic than any other concerned with video games. But most of that ink has been wasted.

The 19th century was infinitely more violent than the 20th in terms of crime (though not actual warfare) and no one played video games. The politicians who have heretofore sent people to war have not played video games—they're too old. The Japanese play video games more than Americans do, as, indeed, they watch more television, but their society is much less violent than America's. No, as we said above, video games are neither good nor bad all by themselves, they neither lead to violence or peace. They can be and do one thing in one family, social, or cultural context, quite another in other such contexts.

If you want to lower violence, then worry about those contexts, which all extend well beyond just playing video games. Politicians who get hot and heavy about violence in video games usually don't want to worry about such contexts, contexts like poverty, bad parenting, and a culture that celebrates greed, war, and winning. Too expensive, perhaps. In my view, the violence and video games question is a silly one and you won't hear more about it here. I do live in fear of people who would kill someone because they have played a video game, but I know that they would equally kill someone if they had read a book or seen a movie or even overheard another nut and I would like you first to take their weapons away. Then, too, someone should have taught these people how to play video games, read books, and watch movies critically and reflectively.

In a world in which millions of people across the globe are dying in real wars, many of them civil wars, it is surely a luxury that we can worry about little boys getting excited for ten minutes after playing a shooter. There are much better things to worry about and I just pray that a time comes in the world where such a problem really merits serious attention. Let's stop the killing, for example in Africa, on the part of people who have never played a video game before we ban games, books, and movies to save ourselves from a handful of disturbed teenagers who would have been better served by better families and schools.

On a more positive note, we should realize that the possibilities of video games and the technologies by which they are made are immense. Video games hold out immense economic opportunities for business and for careers. They hold out equally immense possibilities for the transformation of learning inside and outside schools. They hold out immense promise for changing how people think, value, and live. We haven't seen the beginning yet. As I write, all the game platforms are on their last legs, soon to replaced by more powerful devices. What wonderful worlds will we eventually see? What charged virtual lives will we be able to live?

The Wild West and space were seen new frontiers. Video games and the virtual worlds to which they give birth are, too, a new frontier and we don't know where they will lead. It would be a shame, indeed, not to find out because, like any frontier, they were fraught with risk and the unknown. But, then, I have already admitted that all of us in the complex modern world are frightened of risk and the unknown. But that, I will argue, is a disease of the soul that good games can help alleviate, though, of course, not cure.

I talk about specific games in this book. The danger is that any game can come to seem out of date as newer shiner games appear on the market. But this is a mistake. New games will offer new things (so long as the industry doesn't monopolize), but good older games retain their gaming goodness and we have lots to learn from them. Indeed, we will start with *Castlevania: Symphony of the Night*, a game made for the old *PSOne* and a series with roots in even older game platforms. But *Castlevania: Symphony of the Night* retains all its greatness. It is still a wondrous gaming experience. Gaming is, by historical standards, brand new, but it already has its classics.

After Castlevania, we will move on to other, more contemporary games, games like Full Spectrum Warrior, Thief: Deadly Shadows, The Chronicles of Riddick: Escape from Butcher Bay, Rise of Nations, and The Elder Scrolls III: Morrowind. I have chosen games that I myself like and that I think make my points well. But, there is no shortage of games from which to choose and many others would have done as well. Readers may well like different games than I do, though I would still argue that their pleasures stem from the some of the same sources I discuss here.

Not all my readers will be gamers and that is fine. I am an "old" gamer, an inveterate gamer who came to gaming late. Gamers may find I revel in what they take for granted, like a farmer in the big city for the first time. But then the farmer may see things big city folk have already forgotten. Non-gamers may not share my love for games, but I hope they will share my belief that this is an area of culture than must be taken seriously, especially if am right that we gamers are servicing our souls and recovering our atrophied learning muscles at the same time.

Some people may say, well, he's really arguing it's all about escape from the perils and pitfalls of real life. But, then, I will say there are escapes that lead no where, like hard drugs, and escapes like scholarly reflection and gaming that can lead to the imagination of new worlds, new possibilities to deal with those perils and pitfalls, new possibilities for better lives for everyone. Our emotions and imagination—our souls—need food for the journeys ahead.

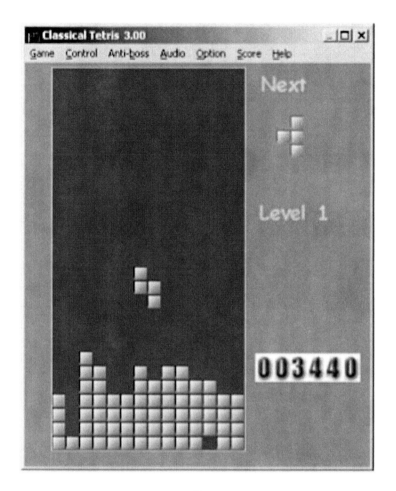

Tetris

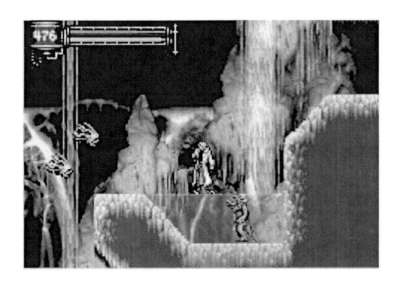

Castlevania

CHAPTER TWO
TETRIS AND *CASTLEVANIA*

TETRIS: PATTERNS AND PLEASURES

Tetris, the most widely played computer game of all time, is a problem-solving puzzle game. Simple geometric shapes each built out of four squares (making shapes like a square, a line like an I, an L shape, a reverse L, and so forth) fall from the top to the bottom of the playing area into a well at the bottom of the screen. The player can manipulate a piece only when it is falling. Falling piece may be rotated, moved horizontally, or dropped to the bottom of the playing area. The player attempts to lock the falling shape smoothly together with the shapes in the well. When blocks are neatly arranged into a solid horizontal row across the playing area, the row is removed from the well and points are scored. The game ends when the pieces stack up to the top of the playing area if and when the player has failed to lock the shapes together into solid rows and remove them before they have risen to the top.

What is the pleasure in *Tetris*? The pleasure is a play between sameness and difference, a play between simplicity and complexity. In *Tetris*, every problem is the same: quickly fitting shapes together into interlocking patterns. And, yet, every problem is different: the exact configuration of shapes being fit together over time varies. The world of *Tetris* looks simple—just falling shapes that can be fit together in various ways—but turns out to be complex. From an obviously simple rule system flows a plethora of complexity (Salin & Zimmerman 2003).

Humans get great pleasure out this sort of play between sameness and difference, between simplicity and complexity. Why? Because we humans are *par excellence* pattern recognizers (Clark 1993; Gee 1992, 2004; Margolis 1987). Finding patterns is what the human mind does best. It's what is most characteristic about our human intelligence. It brings us great pleasure and deep relief.

Finding patterns is almost an obsession with the human mind. People's eagerness and acute ability to find patterns everywhere—sometimes on the basis of slim evidence—is well documented in psychology, anthropology, and evolutionary studies. Among our hunter-gather ancestors—whose genetic tendencies we humans still bear today thanks to the slow pace of evolution—finding and acting on patterns quickly was a matter of survival.

For our ancestors, it really didn't matter if two plants that looked alike were not, in reality, the same sort of plant. If one poisoned you and avoiding both was the price of survival, it was a price well worth paying. After all, hunter-gathers couldn't run any sophisticated chemical tests on plants. It was just as well to treat them both as the same, as falling into the same pattern.

Human being's acute difficulties with correctly thinking about and acting on statistical probabilities are notorious in the literature on human thinking (Shermer 1997). Hunter gatherers didn't have the time or skills to work out mathematical probabilities of being killed by a saber-tooth tiger. In fact, over-reacting to low probability dangerous events probably ensured survival better than "playing the odds" when you had only one life to give in a small band and weren't making policy for the millions who live in today's cities and states.

Sometimes the patterns we humans find are true and meaningful, indeed such patterns often constitute great scientific discoveries, as, for example, in the case of the pattern behind the chemical elements. Sometimes the patterns we "find" are false and meaningless, however reassuring they may still be, as in the case of the patterns astrologists claim to find. Sometimes the patterns we find teeter-totter between truth and falsehood, as in the case of patterns we use to define different cultures, patterns which become dangerous when taken too literally and used without flexibility.

In most cases, the patterns we find are still part and parcel of survival and daily life, such things as family resemblances, the faces of friends, and the patterns behind different types of cuisine (e.g., Chinese cooking), geography (e.g., marshes as against swamps), and work (e.g., the professions). But, of course, we also regularly face worrisome complexities (e.g., problems with government, terrorism across the world, environmental problems) in which we desperately seek to find patterns that we hope will lead to explanations and interventions.

In the normal course of our lives, pattern finding usually works in such a way that we first confront a bevy of complex differences and then seek to find an underlying similarity or sameness among this sea of differences, something that will make sense of the complexity. Say, you have had nothing but problems with a variety of people at work for months. You seek to understand this complex array of difficulties by finding a pattern behind the problems, whether this be other people's jealousy of your superiority, a conspiracy against you, or the weakness of a merit system that pits everyone against everyone else. You can't sleep at night until you find some order, some explanation. Yet you are never really sure the order you find is real and not merely a "just so" story you tell yourself to fall asleep at night.

Tetris works in just the reverse fashion. We first confront a world where everything looks pretty much the same and pretty simple—just falling shapes with interlocking parts. It's quite clear what the rules are. But, as we play, we come to see that this sameness (simplicity) hides a great wealth of different possibilities, different problems and different solutions, a good deal of complexity. In *Tetris*, unlike "real" life, we start from simplicity and discover complexity.

In *Tetris*, a set of simple rules (rules that define a set of shapes, rates of fall, and possible combinations of the shapes) generates a complex array of different problems. Simplicity gives rise to complexity in a quite obvious fashion. In life, we often find ourselves hoping (sometimes vainly) that some set of simple rules exists that will give meaning and order to the complexity we face. In *Tetris* we see clearly that this is the case.

Tetris, thus, models one of our deepest human desires: to solve problems by finding patterns inside a safe world in which there is a clear and comforting underlying order. We see the order (simplicity, pattern) clearly and we safely play among the surprising complexity the game generates always knowing that simplicity and order is there. This sort of event is rare in people's daily lives in the real world. *Tetris* is an escape into the very desire for order, control, and workable solutions that we have all the time in our lives, a desire often frustrated in life, but never in *Tetris*. In *Tetris*, we understand our successes and failures.

It will be one the arguments of this book that video games give humans deep pleasures connected both to the ways in which the human mind works (e.g., we are pattern recognizers *par excellence*) and the ways in which humans now live their lives in our modern, complex, and risky societies. Video games can give human beings on whom their magic works a drug-free high. But I will also argue that just because they fit so well with human minds and offer alleviation from social ills, they also have the capacity—not always realized, of course—to make people more reflective about both thinking and society.

ASSIGNING MEANINGS TO *TETRIS*

While *Tetris* is certainly meaningful in the sense that it offers fulfillment of our desires, it is, in one strict sense of the word, meaningless. The game is simply made up of abstract shapes falling down the screen, at various rates of fall, and locking or failing to lock onto other shapes depending on how the player manipulates them. These shapes and movements carry no particular meanings.

But what would happen if I gave each shape, movement, and combination of shapes in *Tetris* a meaning? For example, let's say I dictate that a given shape in *Tetris* (say the one that looks like an "L") represents a male and another different shape (say the square) represents a female. When either a male shape or a female shape moves towards another such shape, this (I dictate) represents a proposition for sex. If the two shapes lock together (combine with no internal gaps), this (I dictate) means that the proposal for sex has been accepted and if they fail to lock together this means it has been rejected. When the two shapes are locked together, this (I dictate) means they are mating. Now I can say things like, "A female propositioned a male", "The female accepted", and "They mated" (of course, we will get no little baby shapes here).

It isn't hard—though it is silly—to see *Tetris* as all about shapes mating (and since there are many different types of shapes, we could designate more than two genders, creating a world with things beyond males and females). In fact, silly though it be, people have made versions of *Tetris* were the falling shapes are replaced by nude humans contorted into various shapes. The humans fall and can lock together into sexual poses. But we don't need to imagine actually making *Tetris*'s shapes and movements look human, we can just assign them meanings like "male", "female", "mating", and so forth.

If we don't want a pornographic *Tetris*—and I certainly don't—we could change the meanings we have designated. We could make the L shape stand for a king and the square for a queen (and other shapes for other sorts of medieval people). We could make one shape moving towards another mean a proposal of marriage. If the shapes lock together, this could mean the proposal is accepted, if they don't lock together, this could mean the proposal is rejected. Two shapes being locked together would mean they were married.

Of course, we can make the shapes, movements, and combinations mean anything we want them to mean. This is just like creating a little language. After all, it is completely arbitrary, just a matter of convention in the English language, that the string of sounds "bread" means bread in English. In French, that string of sounds doesn't mean anything and the quite different string of sounds "pain" beans bread.

Some people will find this all quite bizarre, because mention of things like kings and queens seems to bring in so many other associations, so much else that is so irrelevant to *Tetris*. Indeed, that will eventually be part of my point, but stick with me for a minute longer.

I could, of course, put a little king crown on the L shape and little queen crown on the square to help people remember the interpretations I have assigned. When a king shape and a queen shape successfully locked together a little heart could appear. I could go on to assign identities and actions to everything else in *Tetris*. Different shapes could be peasants and bishops, clerks and blacksmiths, lords and ladies. If I leave movement as meaning marriage proposals, then the whole game becomes about medieval people and marriage. The old game—with its rule system—is still fully intact. What I have now added, on top of the old rule system, is simply another sort of rule system, a set of rules of how to interpret each of the objects, movements, and combinations in *Tetris*.

Now, all of sudden, each and every move the player makes in *Tetris* produces meanings much like a little language: A queen shape moves towards a king shape means: A queen proposes to a king. The queen and king shapes lock smoothly together means: The king accepts the proposal. The two shapes are together mean: They are married (note nothing stops a queen from marrying a queen, so, too, for kings).

To do such a thing—that is, to assign meanings to each of *Tetris*'s shapes, movements, and configurations—is, as I have already admitted, a pretty silly thing to do. *Tetris* needs no supplement. But, in general terms, what I have done is not as silly as it seems. It turns out not to be silly when we see such a system at work in other games. I imagined this silly thing with *Tetris* simply in order to make the point that one can take a rule system about abstract things like shapes, movements, and combinations and assign the shapes, movements, and combinations meanings.

In fact, all video games are, at bottom, rule systems about shapes (though the shape may look like a person or an object), movements, and combinations. In this sense they are all problem-solving puzzle games and *Tetris* is a pure example. It's just that in many such games, there are interpretations for these shapes, movements, and combinations.

What I have done in my fantasy *Tetris* game is to marry an abstract rule system (*Tetris*'s original rule system) with *story* elements. By "story elements" I mean actors (like kings and queens), actions (like proposing marriage), states (like being married) and events (like a marriage). I call these "story elements" because, after all, stories are composed of such actors, actions, states, and events. After I have done this, my new *Tetris* allows players to generate little story elements as they play the game. I have married rules and story elements in such a way that the rules now produce not just a myriad of problems to be solved (which *Tetris* already did), but simultaneously a myriad of story elements. I have—pretty cheaply— produced a story-element generator from *Tetris*'s rule system.

Note that I am using the term "story elements" here and not the term "story". I am doing so because in no sense does my new *Tetris* generate whole stories of any meaningfulness or depth. It generate actions like "A queen proposes to a king" and states like "The queen and king are married", but nothing like what I would call a whole story, certainly not any very deep or meaningful one.

CASTLEVANIA

A game like *Castlevania: Symphony of the Night* operates pretty much just like my new fantasy version of *Tetris*. In *Castlevania*, like *Tetris*, the player recognizes a relatively simple set of rules about how the virtual object (the virtual character) the joystick controls moves, how that virtual object can interact with other virtual objects in the game, how other objects in the game move, and how spaces in the game world work. The player watches these rules generate a myriad of different problems. But, in this case, each object, movement, and combination that the rules generate is associated with story elements. The virtual character (Alucard in this game) acts, for example, kills a Sword Lord, jumps across an opening, or opens a chest, and gets acted upon, for example, takes damage in a fight, gets poisoned, or even dies. Rules and story elements are married in such a way that one can actually specify or explicate the rule system by specifying the story elements.

Thus, in *Castlevania's* booklet, there is a section entitled "Rules", but the section actually tells *Castlevania's* story:

Castlevania Symphony of he Night

RULES

You are Alucard. Raging through you is the hunger and bloodlust of your vampire father and the gentle empathetic compassion of your human mother. As you have tried to come to terms with that constant internal struggle, you have recognized an outer struggle as well—the need to destroy *Castlevania* and bury the demons both within the castle and within your soul.

On your mission you will discover ancient relics that will open new paths to you. Hidden weapons and magical items from a long time forgotten will be uncovered. Some weapons and items have restricted use—you must earn "hearts" to enable them. As your quest continues, you will encounter myriad monsters and dark forces who will challenge your progress. Every victory gives you experience which yields power and strength. Gradually, you will be able to face and defeat stronger and stronger foes. When you receive damage, you lose some of your life force. Because you are half human you can be defeated more easily than your father. If your life drains to zero, the Start screen will reappear, and (if you have saved a game in progress) you can resume play from the last saved location. (p. 14).

Virtually every part of this story synopsis is just coded talk about the rules of game play. Rather than saying that players should remove ("destroy") any object they come across (as they should lock together any descending shapes in *Tetris*), the text says "you have recognized an outer struggle as well—the need to destroy *Castlevania* and bury the demons both within the castle and within your soul". Now the player is not just removing abstract shapes from the game space, as the player is, indeed, doing, but also defeating demons and destroying objects in Dracula's castle.

The text goes on to explicate, through story elements, how to use special moves (i.e., earn hearts to charge special weapons), how to get your character stronger (i.e., gain experience through killing monsters), what counts as failure (i.e., your life drains to zero), and a variety of other game rules. In *Castlevania*, each shape, movement, and configuration of shapes and movements are assigned meanings in terms of actors, actions, things acted upon, events, and states of affairs.

Thus, just as in our fantasy *Tetris*, in *Castlevania*, as the player uses the rule system (as the player moves, connects, and combines things), the player freely generates story elements (e.g., Alucard kills a Sword Lord; Alucard picks up a gold ring; Alucard jumps in the water). Now players are not just locking one geometrical shape to another, as in *Tetris*. They are killing monsters in Dracula's castle, discovering hidden treasures, or battling specific evildoers attempting to reincarnate Dracula.

Now the text above from *Castlevania* contains something akin to a whole story, but it is important here to be clear on what the role of story is in a game like *Castlevania*. We are so accustomed to stories in books and movies that it is easy to think that stories work the same way in video games like *Castlevania*. They don't.

When we read stories in books and see them in movies we judge them in terms of how interesting their plots (story-lines) are or in terms of what important morals we can draw from them about life. Stories are edifying (we feel uplifted and justified), cathartic (they release our tensions or fears), or informing (we learn something). The story in *Castlevania* does not need to work in any of these ways. If it does, that is just a happy byproduct of the story's primary purpose in *Castlevania*, which is not edification, catharsis, or information, but something else altogether.

The story in *Castlevania* is there to "interpret"—that is, give meaning to—its rule system and, thus, in turn, to interpret and give meaning to each and every action the player takes in the game. It exists so that the player, in playing by the rules, simultaneously generates story elements. The overarching story, which may matter to some players and not others, is not the primary thing. That story is not anything the players themselves have produced. The primary thing here is the player's production, not of a story, but of story elements (e.g., Alucard kills a Sword Lord, Alucard finds a sword shield, Alucard discovers a gold ring, etc.).

Now we might ask: So what? So what that *Castlevania* is a problem solving game (like *Tetris*) in which every object and movement is assigned a meaning? So what that this allows players to freely generate story elements? Why is that important? It is important for several reasons, which I list below, though not in any order of importance, since they are all important and, if one is more important than the others, it is surely the third.

The first answer to our "So what?" question is this: The assignment of meaning to each object, movement, and space in *Castlevania* helps determine what they should look like and sound like (since games have musical scores, as well as various sound effects). Just as saying that a given shape in *Tetris* represents a king suggests we might put a little king crown on the shape, the meaning assignments in *Castlevania* suggest—help generate—the very visual design of the game. The Sword Lord looks the way he does because this object has been assigned the meaning "Sword Lord" in a Dracula universe. There is, of course, still lots of room for what the Sword Lord can look like in detail, but he's not likely to look like an ice-cream cone or an abstract shape. This creates an ambiance for the game. It quite literally gives what is, after all, just an abstract rule system a certain mood, feeling, and look.

Ambiance, mood, feeling, look: these all sound like simple window dressing. But they are important. They are a large part of the pleasure of a game like *Castlevania*. When you (Alucard) walk out on the dark stony ramparts of the castle and see black clouds streaming across a huge full moon, you know what this means, it sends a chill down your spine, it adds a tone to the whole experience, like an important motif in a piece of music.

The original *Castlevania* game for the *Sony PSone* (*Playstation 1*), the game I have been referring to here, is subtitled "Symphony of the Night". And, indeed, moving through such games is like moving through a piece of music where every tone (image) and combination of tones (images) creates moods, feelings, and ambiance, not primarily information (as in movies and books). The experience of playing a game like *Castlevania* is closer to living inside a visual symphony than to living inside a book. And the symphony is not just visual, just composed of images, but it is composed, as well, of sounds, music, actions, decisions, and bodily feelings that flow along as the player-virtual character team act in the game world.

The second answer to our "So what?" question is this: Humans find story-elements profoundly meaningful and are at loss when they cannot see the world in terms of story elements. We try to interpret everything that happens as if it were part of some story, even if we don't know the whole story. We are not just avid pattern recognizers, we humans prefer story-like patterns: this person acted this way because so and so happened; so and so happened because this person acted this way; so-and-so was responsible for this and that. When something happens and we can find no cause or explanation, we are at a loss and deeply unsatisfied. And we humans prefer to find human causes, that is, causes attributable to actors and acts to which we can attribute responsibility in terms of praise or blame.

Say, for example, you find out at work that the boss has fired your best friend and closest colleague. You immediately search for story-elements: my friend is an innocent victim; the boss is an incompetent weakling jealous of my friend's genius; the boss fired my friend because he stood up to the boss at yesterday's committee meeting; my friend has a good legal case against the boss. We assign identities to actors and meanings to their actions and the states to which these actions have given rise. We may not like what happened, but now we can make sense of it. If we find out that none of these events actually makes any sense, that we can assign no story-element values, we are deeply bothered.

The weather has been strange of late; the economy is tanking; traffic is at a stand still; the kids' test scores went down; terrorism is spreading across the globe; there are long lines at all the good restaurants. Here, too, we seek and prefer human causes, actors and actions, individual people to hold innocent or guilty, not larger natural or institutional forces (like "the economy") out of our control and existing at a scale too large and complex for our story-based forms of understanding. We humans are just built that way.

Castlevania allows players to freely generate meaningful acts and events. It allows players to flow through the game always producing obvious sense (Alucard kills a Sword Lord, Alucard moves down the corridor, Alucard destroys a wall, Alucard finds a ring behind the wall, Alucard moves to a portal room, Alucard ports to the front of the castle, Alucard goes to the castle's courtyard, Alucard kills the Owl Knight, etc.). Thanks to the fact that all of the player's actions generate story elements, players are continually acting in the most important sense of acting for humans, that is, in terms of doing meaningful story-like things (actors acting) and bringing about meaningful story-like consequences (this happened because this happened).

Just as *Tetris* allows players to feel continual order and control, *Castlevania* allows them to feel that there is a continual sense of meaning to their actions and the world around them. Many humans feel that actions and events in the real world don't always make much sense or resist the sense we try to make of them, especially in terms of coherent and clearly identifiable actions, reactions, states, and event. This can't happen at the level of game play in *Castlevania*, since every action—thanks to the marriage of story-element assignments and rules—generates meaningful story elements.

So in playing *Castlevania* we are not primarily telling a story, nor reading one either, nor enacting one, though nothing stops us from doing all these things in our minds, should we want to. No, we are primarily generating the materials (elements) out of which all stories are made. The satisfaction here is a pure production of the sorts of meanings (story elements) that most move humans, the sorts of meanings we humans use most consequentially throughout our lives. We produce such meanings in a domain in which there is no shortage and no lack of lucidity. Action becomes transparent in a way in which it never is or rarely is in real life.

This generation of story elements is also part and parcel of the symphony we discussed above. Since all the objects and movements in the game have been assigned values (meanings) and these values have helped generate the visual and auditory design of the game, the actions we players carry out produce more and more of that design. We produce more and more notes that help create the symphony, that give rise to the ambiance, mood, tone, and feel of the "music" we are making. *Castlevania* is an instrument on which the player plays a visual, motoric, auditory, kinesthetic, and decision-making symphony. For example, for me, the look, feel, and flow of Alucard's movements as he jumps across underground springs of water at the bottom of the castle (at a point in the game where water will harm him) while simultaneously breaking Frozen Shades (little blue ice fairies) into ice crystals is one particularly beautiful movement (and moment) in the overall symphony that the playing of *Castlevania* constitutes.

So, *Castlevania* is more like making music than telling a story, reading a book, or watching a movie. But it is music that is made through the player's production of design-generating story-elements. It is like music not at the symphony hall, where everyone sits passively, but music in cultures all across the world where people play instruments, move their bodies, and stomp their feet. The player and the game's designers co-produce a symphony out of the continually rhythmic flow of story-elements integrally connected to visual images, tones, feelings, ambiance, and motoric acts, kinesthetic reactions, and strategic decisions that compose game play as embodied action

TWO STORIES: THE DESIGNER'S STORY AND THE VIRTUAL-REAL STORY.

The third answer to our "So What?" question is this: The marriage of rules and story-element meanings in *Castlevania* allows for two quite different stories to exist in the game. The first story is the one told in the *Castlevania* games (of which there are many). Parts of this story are also given in the booklets that come with the games and on a number of web sites devoted to the games. This is the designer's story (which, of course, gets elaborated and transformed on fan fiction sites).

Below, I give a brief overview of this story as it occurs across the *Castlevania* games (There is much more to the story behind each game than I offer here. The games are listed, not in the order in which they appeared, but in the chronological order of the overall story they tell. I have adapted this material from the following two websites: http://www.gamestyle.net/features.php?feature=77 and http://www.classicgaming.com/*Castlevania*/dungeon.htm):

Castlevania: Lament of Innocence. Playstation 2

It is the 11th century, time of the Crusades. The story focuses on Leon Belmont, a heroic knight. One dark day, his fiancée Sara is kidnapped. His friend, bedridden Mathias Cronqvist (stricken because of the death of his beloved wife), tells Leon that Sara has been taken away by a vampire named Walter. Walter lives in the forest known as Eternal Night and possesses the legendary artifact known as the Crimson Stone. Unable to convince the church to lend him aid, Leon gives up his sword and his title to find Sara himself. Upon entering the evil forest, Leon comes across a mysterious old man named Rinaldo, who gives Leon an enchanted whip.

After making his way to the final chambers of Walter's castle, Leon rescues Sara, only to discover that she has been tainted by the vampire and is doomed. Unable to reverse her cruel fate, Sara sacrifices herself to let her soul be entwined with the enchanted whip, creating the legendary weapon known as the Vampire Killer. The enchanted whip can now destroy the power of Walter on whom Leon takes revenge for the death of his beloved. After defeating the evil vampire, the true nature of the plot is revealed: The kidnapping of Sara was orchestrated by Belmont's friend Mathias. Angry at God for the death of his wife, Mathias sold his soul and embraced the side of the vampire. Mathias then flees, hiding out in other countries under assumed names, slowly working in the underworld and emerging to become Dracula, Lord of the Vampires. Leon swears that, as long as it takes, the Belmont clan will hunt him down and kill him.

Castlevania Legends. Gameboy

In 1450, Sonia Belmont takes up arms to fight Count Dracula as he tries to cover the world in darkness. Underestimated by Dracula, Sonia defeats him and clears his evil from the land. However, because of her power, the people of Romania begin to fear her as much as the Count. This results in Sonia's being exiled from the land.

Castlevania 3: Dracula's Curse. NES

Next comes Sonia's son, Trevor Belmont, who in 1476 comes to the rescue of Romania once again. Since Trevor is the love child of Sonia and Dracula's son with a human mother (Alucard—"Dracula" spelled backwards), he is even more powerful than his mother. Dracula has been awakened by his occultist followers and vows to rid the world of the Belmont family once and for all. However, Trevor gets help from Alucard (who once served his father, but has now changed sides), Grant De Nasty, and vampire hunter Sypha Belnades. Together they dispatch Dracula.

The Castlevania Adventure. Gameboy

In 1576, Dracula rises from his one hundred year entombment believing the Belmonts have ceased to exist long ago. However he is proven wrong when Christopher Belmont appears on the scene to send him back to the grave. Dracula, learning from his last few encounters with Belmonts, realizes he is not match for the Belmonts' power and decides to run and hide until he can develop a more cunning plan to defeat them.

Castlevania 2: Belmont's Revenge. Gameboy

Fifteen years later in 1591, Dracula believes he has a foolproof plan to get rid of Christopher. He takes Christopher' son hostage within his castle. This only serves to enrage Christopher, who storms the castle, finds his son, and rips Dracula apart in a dramatic final encounter, sending him to another one hundred year sleep.

Castlevania - NES; *Castlevania 4* - SNES; *Vampire Killer* - MSX; Castlevania Chronicles – Psone

All these games follow the same story in 1691. This time it is Simon Belmont, the great grandson of Christopher, who must put an end to the evil threatening the land. Trained by a number of great vampire hunters he makes his way through Dracula's castle and defeats him. However it was all as Dracula had planned...

Castlevania 2: Simon's Quest. NES

Because in 1698 Simon finds that in the battle with Dracula he has been put under a curse. The curse will gradually weaken and kill him, so that when Dracula awakens once more there will be no remaining Belmonts around to save the day. Unfortunately for Dracula, Simon has enough strength to gather up Dracula's body parts so that he can not be resurrected—Simon then burns him, thereby lifting the curse.

Castlevania: Harmony of Dissonance. Gameboy Advance

In 1748 Lydie Erlanger, a Transylvanian youngster, has been kidnapped and taken to a castle. Juste Belmont, grandson of Simon, and Maxim Kischine enter to rescue her. Within the castle it transpires that Maxim, in an attempt to prove himself, tries to resurrect Dracula by gathering up his body parts. In the process of doing this, Dracula takes him over and uses him to try and trap Juste. However, Juste, being a Belmont, saves the day and rescues the girl.

Dracula X: Rondo of Blood. SNES, PC Engine

Dracula returns to the idea of kidnapping, when he rises again in 1792. After finding and observing Richter Belmont for some time he decides to kidnap his girlfriend Annette, her sister, Maria, and several other villagers. Fearful of what might happen, Richter sets out with caution to try and save the day. However he soon finds his girlfriend's sister and together they free the remaining captives and destroy Dracula yet again.

Castlevania: Symphony of the Night. Saturn, PSone

In 1797, an evil priest named Shaft decides he wants ultimate power and it is Dracula who was going to give it to him. He places a spell on Richter that causes him to turn to evil. This imbalance in the forces of good and evil causes Alucard to awaken from his self-imposed sleep. Alucard enters the castle and, after meeting with Maria and learning the cause of Richter's defection, kills Shaft and then moves on to defeat his father, Dracula.

Castlevania: Circle of the Moon. Gameboy Advance

All was well until 1830 when the dark priestess Camilla misses her master Dracula so much she decides to resurrect him with the life energy of captured vampire hunter Morris Baldwin. Morris's two young disciples, Hugh Baldwin and Nathan Graves, set out to save him, but soon find out they must not only rescue their teacher, but also stop Dracula from rising from the grave yet again.

Castlevania: Legacy of Darkness. N64

Dracula's followers are getting more proficient in returning him to the land of the living and it only takes until 1844 before a successful resurrection is achieved. However, he is not at full power. He destroys a village in search of the soul of a child to give him back his strength. In doing so he makes a dangerous enemy in the werewolf Cornell who attempts to stop his evil plan. However, though he halts Dracula temporarily, Cornell does not succeed in entombing him again and disappears into history.

Castlevania 64. N64

Which leads to an encounter in 1852 where Reinhart Schneider, Carrie (a descendant of Sypha Belnades), and a knight named Henry, decide it is time that Dracula and his castle are finished off once and for all. After a titanic struggle, they succeed and good is once again restored to the land.

Castlevania Bloodlines. Megadrive/Genesis

In 1914, a witch practicing black magic accidentally revives Dracula's niece, Elizabeth Bartley, who proceeds to attempt to raise Dracula once again. John Morris, a descendant of Quincy Morris (from Bram Stoker's Story), sets out with his friend, Eric LeCarde, knowing the world is depending on them to stop the evil once again.

Castlevania: Aria of Sorrow. Gameboy Advance

Dracula has been resurrected in 1999, but a brave group of warriors has sealed the master of darkness and his evil castle inside a solar eclipse. Though Dracula has been completely destroyed, a new danger begins to rise in 2035. Soma Cruz and his friend Mina Hakuba find themselves transported inside the solar eclipse; inside they meet a cult leader named Graham who is intent on gaining the powers of Dracula. Soma must stop him and find out why he has been summoned to the land of *Castlevania*.

This story—the designer's story—is the story that I have already said is not primary, though certainly some players love it and are very motivated to play the game because of it. The player has not made this story up, the games' designers have. As far as game play goes, in a game like *Castlevania*, this story exists primarily to allow the assignment of story-elements to the objects and movements in the game, to marry rules and story-elements. In that sense, it exists, as well, primarily to allow for a second sort of story to exist.

This second story is crucially important. Every player of *Castlevania* who does everything you can do in the game will, in the end, have done all the same things. A player who does less will have done some sub-set of this. This is just like a book. Everyone who reads the whole book will have read the same text. Any reader who reads less will have read some sub-set of this whole text.

However, each player of *Castlevania* will have done and found things in entirely different orders and in different ways from each other. Players will have ventured into the parts of the castle in different orders, they will have revisited them a different number of time. They will have faced the bosses in the game at different times and will have defeated them in different ways and with different degrees of difficulty in doing so. They will have found key items in the game in different orders. They will have made different choices of what strategies to use, when to save, and what equipment to wear and use. This is to say that each player has enacted a different *trajectory* through the game.

There is no sense of different trajectories in a game like *Tetris*. What allows us to feel and recognize a different trajectory in a game like *Castlevania* is, of course, the story-elements. We can recognize that this distinctive event (e.g., Alucard killed his first Sword Lord) happened before or after another distinctive event (Alucard found the gold ring). Story-elements give the player a way to mark time and against this marking each player comes to see that they have enacted a unique trajectory through the game space.

This trajectory has an important consequence. Your Alucard is different than my Alucard. Yours has a different trajectory than mine. This means that the virtual character in the game world—Alucard in this case—is different for each player in a significant and meaningful way.

The hero is, thus, not Alucard from the designer's story, nor you the real-world player (you are, after all, playing Alucard). It is "Alucard-you", a melding of the virtual character, Alucard, and you, the real-world player who has steered Alucard on a unique trajectory through the game.

The hero in my personal trajectory through the game was "Alucard-Jim", a blend between a virtual (Alucard) and real person (me). This is why players can so readily switch between saying "Alucard killed the Sword Lord" and "I killed the Sword Lord". The real actor here is a composite or blend: Alucard-you (me).

This trajectory is the second story. Let's call it, to distinguish it from the designer's story, the "virtual-real story", because it is the story enacted by a blend of the virtual character (Alucard, in this case) and the real-world player. This is the important story in *Castlevania*. Players can play the game over again to gain another trajectory—good games lend themselves to such re-play, to the building of new trajectories. This trajectory is personal and individual in a game like *Castlevania*. It can be both personal and social in a multiplayer game.

So when I play *Castlevania*, not only do I freely generate story elements and not only do I co-produce a visual-motoric-auditory symphony, I also generate a unique story—this second story, the virtual-real story. It is the story of my own unique trajectory through the game world. This story is the tale of Alucard-Jim and I can lard it up with all the fantasies, values, and morals I want to—no permissions needed, no critics allowed.

In the Alucard-Jim story, Alucard-Jim was only able to beat the large knight with the owl on his shoulder at the front of the castle (the Owl Knight) after Alucard-Jim became more powerful (Alucard by gaining experience and Jim by getting more practice and skill). For some other player, let's say "Joe", Alucard-Joe had a much easier time killing the Owl Knight early on with less hassle and effort than did Alucard-Jim. Alucard-Jim had tried unsuccessfully several times earlier to kill the Owl Knight. After Alucard and Jim had gained experience, Alucard-Jim proudly marched to the front of the castle and, with great glee, mastered him easily.

This event (Alucard-Jim finally kills the Owl Knight at the front of the castle) became one of my own unique high points in the symphony I was co-producing, the symphony I was performing with the designers' "score" (rules married to story elements)—because, though the designer owns the designer's story, I own the Alucard-Jim story, the virtual-real story. Joe has different high points, because he has a different virtual-real story.

Each of us human beings has a unique trajectory through life. Indeed, the trajectory (second story) I am talking about in *Castlevania* is much more similar to our own life trajectories than it is to the linear and intricately pre-designed stories in books and movies. *Castlevania* is a little second life, much safer, saner, more ordered, and more understandable than real life. The game offers the pleasures of making a life—of making our own trajectory (but a virtual-real one)—without the fears and pains. We would all like to see our own lives as beautiful symphonies of meaning we are performing, but often can't. It is easy to see *Castlevania* this way.

There is also another story relevant to *Castlevania*, though not as relevant to my concerns here, and that is the real-world player's story of game playing as a real-world activity, in this case, "Jim's story". This story has things in it like "Jim played *Castlevania* late into the night", "Jim sometimes got angry when his character died right before getting to a save room", "Jim stopped playing the game *Sacred* to devote more time to playing *Castlevania*", "Jim played *Castlevania* in his office/study at home", and so forth. These are real-world events involving the real-world actor Jim. Admittedly, they can and do bleed into the virtual-real story (which is the story of Alucard-Jim in a blended virtual-real world), especially in the case of emotions like "Alucard-Jim killed the Owl Knight with great glee", but the two stories are easy enough to distinguish at a conceptual level. "Jim's story" exists outside the game, while the virtual-real story mixes the outside world of Jim and the inside world of Alucard.

We will move on now to other types of video games. But we should not forget or take for granted the deep pleasures of games like *Tetris* and *Castlevania*. The other games we will discuss, though they will look quite different and will, indeed, be quite different, nonetheless, deep down retain some of the pleasures of *Tetris* and *Castlevania*, though not in their pure form. But first, in the next chapter we will meditate briefly on what implications a games like *Tetris* and *Castlevania* might hold out for learning in our complex, modern societies.

CHAPTER THREE
CASTLEVANIA AND LEARNING

At first sight, it certainly looks as if something as pleasurable as playing *Castlevania: Symphony of the Night* has nothing to do with anything so ponderous as "learning". This is because school has made many people believe that pleasure and learning have nothing to do with each other. But this is untrue. Learning is a deep human need, like mating and eating, and like all such needs, it is meant to be deeply pleasurable to human beings. So the real paradox is not that pleasure and learning go together, but, rather, how and why school manages to separate them.

Harry Harlow, a psychologist famous for his studies on baby monkeys' deep need for bodily contact with their mothers early in life, did early intelligence testing on monkeys (Blum 2002). Following the established paradigm of such research, Harlow coaxed the monkeys to solve complicated puzzles by giving them food rewards for each step of the puzzle. One day, however, Harlow wondered what the monkeys would do if they were confronted with the puzzles, but given no food rewards. He predicted they would stop at the first step if they received no rewards.

But the monkeys did no such thing. They worked on the problems, and solved them, just as eagerly and readily as when they had received food rewards. For the monkeys, learning was a reward in and of itself, a reward powerful enough to keep them happily going at problem solving for long stretches of time. If this is true of monkeys, how much truer is it of human beings, who can and need to learn even more than other primates?

So what is a player learning when playing *Castlevania: Symphony of the Night*? How to play the game, of course. And how to solve its problems. This game, like all good video games, offers players continual opportunities to learn, solve problems, and become more skilled. That is, indeed, what makes such games fun. Humans, at least out of school, like to learn, solve problems, and get more skilled.

So what can we learn about school-type learning from a game like *Castlevania: Symphony of the Night*? What can we learn, for instance, about learning something like science, say biology (it doesn't really matter what content domain we take as an example; it could be any area of science or any area of the humanities or social sciences)? First, we can learn this: if you want someone to learn anything, biology say, make the learning a game-like enterprise that teaches a person how to play it by playing it.

Furthermore, make the very basis of the pleasure in the game continual opportunities for learning, problem solving, and becoming more skilled. Tap into the human need, drive, desire for—and pleasure in—learning. Of course, this need, drive, desire, and pleasure may have already been killed or at least sent into deep hibernation by previous schooling. This damage will have to be undone before healthy learning can occur.

When I say "game-like enterprise", I don't mean we have to have people learning biology or any other such thing from an actual game, though there is nothing wrong with this idea. I mean we should have learners engaged in actions and activities that share features with good video games. Let's see what some of these are in the case of a game like *Castlevania: Symphony of the Night*. We will see other sorts of features connected to other sorts of games in later chapters.

We have seen that *Castlevania: Symphony of the Night* allows players to create their own visual, kinesthetic, auditory, actional symphonies: a set of motifs flowing through time in a wondrous and beautiful way is produced by the player's own actions and decisions. This unique symphony creates the ambiance, mood, and feeling of the game, the affectual backdrop that far from being peripheral to the game, is absolutely central to its pleasures. We saw that this happens because a game like *Castlevania* is designed in such a way that a simple rule system about shapes, movements, and connections among them is married to story elements, namely actors, actions, states, and events. These actors, actions, states, and events have a certain look and feel that is continually produced by the player's movement through the game.

Players can create these symphonies of form, sound, and movement because the game's designers have offered them a rich palette of resources from which to build them through their own choices and actions. The story elements the designers have chosen to marry to their rule system give rise to the particularly distinctive images and sounds that then compose the game— in the case of *Castlevania: Symphony of the Night*, these are images and sounds from the realm of Dracula. In turn, players freely generate these image and sounds via their unique trajectories through the game, composing their own visual-auditory-actional symphonies.

Research in cognitive science, the science that studies human learning, has shown quite clearly that feeling and emotion are not peripheral to thinking and learning, but central to them (Damasio 1995, 2003). If humans add affect (feeling and emotion—in a sense, caring) to information as they process it, they store this information in their mind/brains far more deeply and connect it far more integrally to their other knowledge than if they process it without any such affectual colorings.

If learners are to learn biology deeply—or any other area—then they need to feel and care about the world of biology in which they are "playing" (in the game-like experience we are giving them). So here, too, as in

Castlevania, learners need to be offered a rich palette of resources from which they can build their own symphonies to create the all important ambiance, mood, and feeling of the game of biology they are playing or the world of biology in which they are acting and living.

A player's actions and decisions in *Castlevania: Symphony of the Night* creates a colorful and affect-laden world, a world which recruits the player's feelings, emotions, and interest in powerful ways. So, too, in doing biology, a learner's actions and decisions should create a colorful and affect-laden world that recruits the learner's care, feelings, emotions, and interest. Unfortunately, this background of affect—of feeling, emotion, caring, interest, and excited expectation about what will come next—is treated as entirely unimportant in school. Nonetheless, it is the background without which there is no real learning. Without it, deep pleasure is not triggered, and pleasure is central to learning.

We have also seen that games like *Castlevania* create a unique trajectory through the game for each player—what we called the second story or the virtual-real story. This happens because the player-character's actions produce story-elements like "Alucard killed a Sword Lord". Players can, thus, date when they have done different things, can track their progress, can tell their own unique story of how they got through. This unique trajectory makes it *my own* experience, *my own* story, creates a powerful sense of ownership. I remember how hard it was to kill my first Sword Lord. I remember how I felt when I and my character finally successfully confronted the Owl Knight at the front of the castle.

But this happens only because of the way in which the real-world player (me) blends with the virtual character (Alucard). Alucard is my surrogate body in the virtual world. We are a joint actor. He allows me to act in a world (the virtual world, Castlevania) into which I cannot bring my real-world body, try as hard as I may to walk into the screen.

Learners of biology in school aren't really biologists. When they start, the world of biology is very much like a virtual world they do not have the power to walk into by themselves. They cannot all by themselves accomplish biological deeds. They are "lay" people and they, too, need a surrogate— another identity—with which to enter the world of biology. They need to be helped to take on an identity as some type of biologist who is going to play (do) biology, live and act in a world designed by the values of biologists (diSessa 2000).

Designers (teachers) need to create a game-like biology world in which learners can act and decide as certain types of biologists, not just as real-world lay people. They need to offer learners an identity and tools with which to enter and play in that world. They need to marry the rules of this world with story elements in such a way that learners can continually produce story elements ("learner-as-a-certain-type-of-biologist does such-and-such") in terms of which they can date and track their own unique progression through that world. Learners need to own the game of biology they are playing as deeply as they own *Castlevania* when they have finished it.

But, of course, children in school rarely live in the worlds—like biology—they study. They rarely feel ownership of these worlds based on powerful identities they have taken on in them. They sit passively and watch teachers feed them loads of facts and information about animals and nature. This is just as senseful and pleasurable as sitting for a bunch of facts about *Castlevania: Symphony of the Night* without being able to play it.

Biology is not a set of facts. It is not pieces of information. It is a set of activities, connected to certain sorts of identities, values, ambiance, and feelings, that productively *generate* facts and information and lots more— images, symbols, equations, theories, stories, experiments, fields trips, dialogue. It is a set of symphonies produced by people who know how to play the game. In this case, these symphonies are often collaboratively produced. Biology is often not a single-player game. But each player who produces biological knowledge, as a biologist and not just a "lay" person, has his or own trajectory through the biology game and a feeling of ownership based on this personal trajectory. For each, biology of the type for which they have a passion has a certain feel and gives a deep pleasure.

Biology or any other area of study is not a direct reflection of the real world. The real world can be described from many different perspectives. Biology, like all sciences, offers models of the world. Models are theories about how the world works. They are very often simulations (on paper, computers, or in scientists' heads) of some part of the real world. These models, theories, or simulations are always simplifications of the real world. A blow-by-blow description of the real world that captured every possible fact would be impossible and useless in any case because too long and detailed.

These models, theories, or simulations are created by people with certain interests, skills, values, and identities. Other sorts of models, theories, and identities (e.g., in physics) are created by other sorts of people. Some models, theories, or simulations work better than others at making predictions about the real world. For instance, astronomy works better than astrology. No model, theory, or simulation works perfectly, none works for every aspect of reality. The creation of these models, theories, or simulations is a product of *work* accomplished by people who have learned the skills and taken on the identities of model builders, theory builders, simulations builders in their chosen areas. But for these people, this work is much more akin to play than it is to work, at least in terms of how many others in our society and in our schools view work.

There is no reason whatsoever why biology in school needs to be less pleasurable, less connected to play, less tied to ownership, less a beautiful symphony of images and actions that *Castlevania*. In school, too, learners can blend with a new identity—for example, an emergent biologist of a certain type—and, combining their real world identities and cultures with this new way of thinking, acting, feeling, and talking, produce their own new story of their trek through biology.

I say there is no reason, but, of course, there is. Game-like learning cannot be incorporated into our schools unless those schools make radical changes. As long as they stay skill-and-drill testing centers preparing most kids with "basic skills" for service jobs, while allowing a few rich kids, with no real ability, to apply their knowledge to get A's for passing fact-based tests, they will resist such learning. Worse, they will co-opt any attempts to use such learning into their own agenda. *Jeopardy* and *Trivial Pursuit* will be the games of choice in school.

Full Spectrum Warrior

Thief

Riddick

CHAPTER FOUR
FULL SPECTRUM WARRIOR, THIEF, AND RIDDICK

CASTLEVANIA: GAMERS AND VAMPIRE HUNTERS

We have seen that the important story in *Castlevania* is not the designer's story, but a second story. This second story is the trajectory that Alucard and I—Alucard-Jim—have taken through the game. This is the Alucard-Jim story, a virtual-real story.

What skills do Alucard and Jim need and use to get through a game like *Castlevania* and accomplish the Alucard-Jim story? Well, both of us need and use relatively generic action-game skills.

Alucard walks, runs, jumps, blocks, and attacks in ways that are typical of a great many video games, including many games that are about quite different things. For instance, Mario in a game like *Super Mario* for the *Nintendo 64*, also walks, runs, jumps, and attacks, though in a quite different looking world. Sonic the Hedgehog in a game like *Sonic Adventure 2 Battle* for the *Nintendo GameCube* could hardly be more different from Alucard. He moves (dashing and rolling) and fights in a different style, but, nonetheless, his skills still consist in a basic set of movements and interactions that are versions of walk, run, jump, and attack. These are the typical game action skills that many virtual characters in games have.

When I play *Castlevania* I, like Alucard, call on my rather generic action-gaming skills, skills that I use in one form or another in a great many other games. I push buttons to make Alucard walk, run, block, or attack. Timing and combining the buttons in certain ways can be important. Like many other video game characters, Alucard can do some special moves when I push two buttons at once. These are the typical action skills that many games require real-world players to have.

The point is that in games like *Castlevania*, players compose a symphony of images and actions from a simple set of button pushes on the controller. This symphony is enacted by a virtual character (e.g., Alucard) who engages in a simple set of movements, actions, and interactions. The fact that this simplicity gives rise to beauty and complexity is what makes a game like *Castlevania*—just like *Tetris*—so entrancing. After all there are only three buttons on a trumpet, but it is an instrument that can make an endless array of different music.

However, we need to note that Alucard has different game skills than I do. He knows how to move and fight in the game world, while I know how and when to order him to do so. I also control Alucard's timing, though he controls his own execution of his attacks, which he varies depending on the weapon with which I have equipped him. So Alucard and I have different (action) game skills—different game relevant action abilities—but we need to combine and coordinate these to play the game well and to succeed at it. Alucard and Jim have to get their act together to succeed.

The blend Alucard-Jim, which looks like a double blend, is actually a triple blend: Alucard and Jim are yoked together through the fact that they each have only some of the game skills necessary to play the game. Let's call these game skills, parts of which Alucard has and parts of which I have and which become a coherent system only when they get combined, "gaming expertise". Thus, the double blend Alucard-Jim is really the triple blend: Alucard ←gaming expertise → Jim. I place an arrow pointing to each player to notate that the gaming expertise is parceled out between Alucard and Jim, neither of whom has the whole set needed to play the game.

We can see now how we can get to a very different sort of game than *Castlevania*, if we consider one of Alucard's and Jim's limitations in a game like *Castlevania*, however much this limitation is, in fact, part of the beauty of the game. Alucard is a vampire hunter. When I play him, I am playing as a vampire hunter. However, even though Alucard is a vampire hunter, he has no distinctive skills associated with this profession. As I have said, he has pretty much the same skills as Mario, or Sonic for that matter, though Mario and Sonic are no vampire hunters.

As a player of *Castlevania*, I need not develop or use any skills distinctive of a vampire hunter, either. While images from vampire lore are important to the game, and while I may imagine all sorts of things about vampires while playing the game, the game does not demand that I emulate the vampire hunter's professional ways of thinking and acting.

The reason for this—for the fact that both Alucard and I draw only on gaming skills to enact our trajectory through the game and not professional vampire hunter skills—is that *Castlevania* has married simple story elements (single actors and actions) to an abstract rule system (about shapes, movements, and combinations). So while the game can generate story elements, it cannot generate other things. It cannot, for instance, generate the professional practice of a vampire hunter.

Why not? Because the professional practice of a vampire hunter—like the professional practice of any other professional—is not composed only of simple actions of certain types, though it is, of course, partly composed of these (and a game like *Castlevania* has no trouble allowing distinctive vampire-hunter actions like plunging a silver stake into a vampire's heart as a way to kill the vampire). A professional practice (whether of a vampire hunter or a modern doctor) is composed, as well, of distinctive sorts of knowledge, values, practices, and strategies. Strategies are chains of actions connected and integrated in planned ways on the basis of the professional's distinctive knowledge and values. *Castlevania* can't generate knowledge, values, or any deep strategies tied to the distinctive professional knowledge and values of a vampire hunter. It's just not built that way. It isn't intended to do that.

To win *Castlevania*, I have to think like a gamer, not like a professional vampire hunter. Now I must admit that I personally have no idea what the professional values, knowledge, and practices of vampire hunters are. And *Castlevania* makes no attempt to emulate these, nor to teach them to players.

Things are different in a game like *Full Spectrum Warrior* for the *Xbox*. This game teaches the player how to be, albeit not a professional vampire hunter, but a professional soldier. It demands that the player thinks, values, and acts like one to "win" the game. You cannot bring just your game playing skills—the skills you use in *Castlevania*, *Super Mario*, or *Sonic Adventure 2 Battle* to this game. You do need these, but you need another set of skills, as well, to play the game. And these additional skills are, in fact, a version of the professional practice of modern soldiers, specifically, in this game, the professional skills of a soldier commanding a dismounted light infantry squad composed of two teams.

Before we proceed though I need to clarify two things. First: I will be use the word "professional" below. This word carries a lot of baggage I don't want and don't intend. After my discussion of *Full Spectrum Warrior*, I will discuss what I want to mean and don't want to mean by the word "professional". For the moment, however, I think that just leaving the word as it is will make the following discussion clearer for the reader and prepare the reader for the later cautions I will make the word.

Second: I am about to discuss the game *Full Spectrum Warrior*. I am well aware that this game is ideologically laden. I am well aware that it carries messages, beliefs, and values about war, warfare, terrorism, cultural differences, the U.S. military, and the role of the U.S. and its army in the modern, global world. I myself don't agree with some of these messages, beliefs, and values. But all that needs to be left to the side for now. It is not that these issues are not important. However, right now, our only mission is to understand the game *Full Spectrum Warrior* as an example of a particular type of game. Without such understanding, critique would be superficial at best in any case.

FULL SPECTRUM WARRIOR

In *Full Spectrum Warrior*, the player controls two (sometimes three) squads of four soldiers each. The player uses the buttons on the controller to give orders to the soldiers, as well as to consult a GPS device, radio for support, and communicate with command. The Instruction Manual that comes with the game makes it clear from the outset that players must think, act, and value like a professional soldier to play the game successfully:

> You command a dismounted light infantry squad, a highly trained group of soldiers who understand how to operate in a hostile, highly populated environment. Everything about your squad—from the soldiers to its equipment to its tactics—is the result of careful planning and years of experience on the battlefield. Respect that experience, soldier, since it's what will keep your soldiers alive. (p. 2)

No such thing—having to think, act, and value like a professional (e.g., vampire hunter)—is found in a game like *Castlevania*. But there is something else here that is new, as well. We have seen that in the second story in *Castlevania*, the important story, the virtual-real story, the game is played by Alucard-Jim. We have also seen that neither Alucard nor Jim incorporates any depth of professional knowledge about vampire hunting into his skill set. However, in *Full Spectrum Warrior* both the character the player manipulates (the soldiers on the squads) and the player him or herself knows (or comes to know) professional military practice. As the manual says, the soldiers "understand how to operate in a hostile, highly populated environment" and the player learns this or fails at the game.

Full Spectrum Warrior is designed in such a way that certain sorts of professional knowledge and certain types of professional skill are built right into the virtual characters, the soldiers (and into the enemies, as well). The game is also designed to teach players some of the attitudes, values, practices, strategies, and skills of a professional officer commanding a squad. For instance, consider what the manual has to say about "Moving Your Soldiers":

> Moving safely in the environment is the most important element of successful command. The soldiers on your teams have been trained in movement formations, so your role is to select the best position for them on the field. They will automatically move to the formation selected and take up their scanning sectors, each man covering an arc of view. (p 15)

Note, again, the value statement here: "Moving safely in the environment is the most important element of successful command". I guarantee you that, in this game, if you do not live and play by this value, you will not get far in the game. You'll just spend all your time carrying wounded soldiers back to CASEVACs, because of another value the game demands: "The U.S. Army has zero tolerance for causalities!". This value is enforced by the very design of the game, since if even one of your soldiers dies, the game is over and you have lost:

> When a solider is shot, he may become incapacitated. When this happens, a skull icon will appear in his slot on the D-pad. You have a limited time in which you can give aid to the wounded soldier before he dies, indicated by the skull icon losing color. If you don't give aid to the soldier before the time runs out, he will die and you will fail your mission. The U.S. Army has zero tolerance for causalities! (p. 25).

But note also that your soldiers, the virtual characters in the game (like Alucard in *Castlevania*), actually have professional knowledge built into them: "The soldiers on your teams have been trained in movement formations, so your role is to select the best position for them on the field. They will automatically move to the formation selected and take up their scanning sectors, each man covering an arc of view". In turn, the game demands that you, the player, attain such knowledge, as well: "your role is to select the best position for them on the field".

There are lots of things your soldiers know and lots of things you, the player, needs to come to know. However, these are not always the same things. That is, your soldiers know different things than you know, they have mastered different bits of professional military practice than the bits you need to master to play the game. For example, they know how to take a variety of different formations and you need to know when and where to order them into each such formation. You yourself do not need to know how to get into such formations (e.g., in the game you don't place each solider in position—on the order, they assume the formation as a group).

As another example of the way in which knowledge is parceled out between you and your troops in this game, consider ways of moving your soldiers from one position to the next in hostile territory. There two ways to do this, one is called "rushing" and the other is called "bounding":

> The standard press version [single push of the A button, JPG] of a move order is the Rush. It is the fastest way to move since all four soldiers move toward the destination simultaneously. Well trained U.S. soldiers never fire a weapon without stopping their movement and going sighted (raising the gun to a firing position). In other words, Rushing soldiers never fire

while moving, so they will not engage targets until they finish the move and you issue a fore order.

The hold version [hold the A button down] of a move order is the Bounding Overwatch or Bound. Bounding is the safest way to move when your team is going into unknown territory or moving against one or more enemies that are close together because your soldiers are sighted and return fire as they move.

Issuing a bound order has two steps. First you press and hold the A button while the movement cursor is out to order the bound. This automatically opens the fire sector cursor so you can set the area for your soldiers to cover. Pressing the A button again completes the Bound order.

Once they receive a Bound order, the soldiers will move into position. The first two soldiers will start toward the destination while the rear two soldiers provide cover fire. Once the first two soldiers finish their movement, they cover the rear soldiers' move. When soldiers fire while Bounding, they automatically suppress to keep the target's head down.

Note that Bounding is very unsafe if there are enemies who are too far apart to be in the same fire sector. If you Bound under these circumstances, you are very likely to lose one of your soldiers. (p. 16).

Note, once again, the values: "Well trained U.S. soldiers never fire a weapon without stopping their movement and going sighted (raising the gun to a firing position)". Note, again, as well, the parceled out knowledge. Your soldiers know how to rush and bound (and they will abide by the value of not firing without stopping and going sighted). You need to know when to rush and when to bound and what area to have your bounding soldiers cover (i.e., to be prepared to stop and fire at if they see any enemies in the area). Note, too, the strategic knowledge that is needed: "Note that Bounding is very unsafe if there are enemies who are too far apart to be in the same fire sector. If you Bound under these circumstances, you are very likely to lose one of your soldiers".

Of course, most of the knowledge, values, strategies, and skills the player picks up in this game, he or she picks up, not from reading the manual, which is, after all, only a small booklet, but from playing the game. The game has a tutorial, hints, and much in its design that helps players learn the knowledge, values, practices, strategies, and skills necessary to be enact professional military knowledge and play the game well.

What we see here is important—we have left the world of *Tetris* and *Castlevania*—not for a better world, but for a different one. A game like *Full*

Spectrum Warrior requires more than generic gamer knowledge and skills, it requires professional knowledge and skills, as well, but this professional military knowledge is parceled out, shared between, the virtual characters and the player, each of whom knows some things in common, but different things as well. The technical term for a situation like this, where parts of a coherent knowledge domain (like military knowledge) are parceled out in this way, is to say that the knowledge is *distributed* (Hutchins 1995).

What this distribution of professional knowledge amounts to is the creation of a third story, a story that does not exist in a game like *Castlevania*. In a game like *Full Spectrum Warrior* there is, as in *Castlevania*, the first story, the designer's story. In this game, the designer's story is about a fictitious country called "Zekistan":

> After the U.S.-led operations in Afghanistan and Iraq, thousands of ex-Taliban and Iraqi loyalists crossed the borders of Zekistan seeking asylum by invitation of the nation's dictator, Al Afad. It wasn't long before the same terrorist training facilities and death-camps that the U.S. fought to remove in Afghanistan were operating again under full sponsorship by Al Afad's government. After repeated warnings and failed diplomatic resolutions in the UN, NATO votes to invade Zekistan to depose Al Afad, eliminate the terrorist element, and stop the ethnic cleansing of the Zeki people. (p. 8)

As in *Castlevania*, this story—the designer's story—is not the primary one. As in *Castlevania*, there is a second story in *Full Spectrum Warrior*, a story that is more important. This is the trajectory through the game each player takes, a trajectory that is different for each player. Each player has taken different routes, made different choices, and done some things in a different order. This second story—this unique trajectory—is the accomplishment, not of the virtual characters (the soldiers) alone or of the player (Jim) alone, but of the blend of these two, the virtual characters and real-world player, the equivalent of Alucard-Jim in *Castlevania*, here soldiers-Jim. This is the virtual-real story.

But now there is a third story or, if you prefer, the second story, the trajectory, transmutes into a quite different type of story. This third story goes beyond just where I (the player) have been and what I've done in the game (the second story). This third story is the story of the soldiers and Jim's enactment of professional knowledge. In *Castlevania*, Alucard and Jim share no professional knowledge or practice. But in *Full Spectrum Warrior*, the soldiers (virtual characters) and Jim do share such knowledge and practice. They have distributed knowledge of military values, strategies, practices, and skills. This fact gives rise to a different sort of trajectory through the game, a third story.

This is the story of *our career* (the soldiers and me) as military professionals. Each player has made different strategic military choices, engaged in different military tactics, enacted military values in different places and different ways, succeeded and failed at different places and tasks with military significance. Once again, these choices have been enacted by the player blended with the virtual characters, the soldiers—a blend that is fully necessary here, since military knowledge is distributed between these two.

The second story here (a player's trajectory through the game in terms of the order in which he or she has gone places and done things) and the third story (the soldiers and my career in terms of the progressive joint deployment of professional military knowledge), of course, blend together and are only usefully distinguished for analytical purposes. The point is that *Castlevania* has a second story (the Alucard-Jim's story), while *Full Spectrum Warrior* has this (soldiers-Jim's story) in terms of both a different trajectory through game space (as in *Castlevania*) and a different trajectory through the deployment of military knowledge in the game space (a "career").

Another equally good way to say this is that in a game like *Full Spectrum Warrior* a career has been overlayed on top of the second story, the trajectory of the player's movement through the game. If a game like *Castlevania* allows a unique trajectory through the game for each player, a game like *Full Spectrum Warrior* allows a unique military career through the game for each player.

In the career story of my soldiers and I, I remember solving a particular problem by calling in air support at a crucial moment. At a similar moment in the game, in the career of your soldiers and you, you remember out-flanking the opposition so that you needed no air support, though this meant one of your soldiers got wounded and this, in turn, necessitated a nerve wracking trip back to the CASEVAC.

In one particular campaign I engaged in one set of related strategies, faced some failures, but eventually came through. In that campaign, you engaged in a different set of related strategies, faced no real problems, and came throw with flying colors. You and I have had different professional careers by the time we have finished the game. We can sit by the fireside and tell different war stories—professional stories—of our professional military feats and expertise.

What a game like *Full Spectrum Warrior* adds to the gaming space, something that is not in games like *Castlevania*, is a shared professional role and distributed knowledge between the virtual character (or characters) and the real-world player. It is as if *Castlevania* had created such a shared role and distributed knowledge for Alucard and Jim in terms of the values, knowledge, practices, strategies, and skills of a professional vampire hunter. The game would have to have built such knowledge into Alucard and into me and created a world that allowed for the creative expression and enactment of such knowledge so that each player of the game could have had a different professional career (used different strategies) as a vampire hunter.

This would have made *Castlevania* a very different game. And, indeed, *Castlevania* needs no such transformation. It is a wonderful game in its own right. Its pleasures are all its own and we have discussed these pleasures in Chapter 2. But *Full Spectrum Warrior* is a wonderful game, as well, and a very different one. Its pleasures are its own, as well. And what exactly are these pleasures?

We have argued, in Chapter 2, that one of the deep pleasures of games like *Tetris* and *Castlevania* is the feeling of control and order that these games allow—in both games we start with simplicity and find a controlled and well-ordered complexity. We have argued, as well, that *Castlevania* allows the free production of story elements and that such story elements are the sorts of meanings and patterns humans find most satisfying. So *Castlevania* is a site of constantly flowing, fluid, transparent meanings (Alucard-I acts). But *Full Spectrum Warrior* allows players to feel control, order, and meaning in a different way. It allows them to experience *expertise*, to feel like an expert.

Few people in our society get to become experts in important domains. In fact, they must spend most of their time trusting experts, all the while aware of how often the world doesn't behave the way the experts say it should or will. Experts claim to have special knowledge and skills that allow them a very special sort of control over complexity, beyond the control everyday people can experience. It is easy to see why someone fighting in a war would want to believe that there is a body of expertise in terms of knowledge, skills, and experience that can make them and their friends safer in a very unsafe setting. And, indeed, however tenuous such expertise may sometimes be, it is far better than being a rank amateur on the battlefield, a fate that leaves one feeling the victim of caprice.

Games like *Full Spectrum Warrior* allow players to participate in expert knowledge, values, strategies, and skills. They allow players to experience a sense of control—a partial (but only partial) control over fate and caprice—in a complex and sometimes dangerous and threatening set of situations. Players experience a certain expert mastery of complexity, risk, and danger. Such a feeling—often quite lacking in real life—is exhilarating.

A game like *Full Spectrum Warrior* produces not just story elements like *Castlevania* (Alucard killed a Sword Knight), it produces, as well, what we might call "professional career story moments", for example, things like "Squad Alpha out-flanked a machine gun nest". So here we get not just constantly flowing, fluid transparent meanings in terms of simple acts, but constantly flowing, fluid meanings that interpret these simple actions in terms of professional knowledge, values, strategies, and skills. These professional meanings are, for the most part, much more transparent in a video game than they are in real life (or real warfare). In real life it is not always clear whether a given strategy worked, why it worked, or even exactly what it was. These matters are usually clearer—partly thanks to clearer outcomes—in a video game.

So if we see *Castlevania* as marrying a set of story elements to an abstract rule system, we can see *Full Spectrum Warrior* as marrying professional knowledge, values, strategies, and skills to these story elements. *Full Spectrum Warrior* organizes the story elements into strategic sets (i.e., "outflank" is a higher order strategic action made up of a good many other simpler actions) in such a way that they come to generate professional practices, not just simple acts.

We argued above that in a game like *Castlevania* the blend Alucard-Jim, which looks like a double blend, is actually a triple blend: Alucard and Jim are yoked together through the fact that they each have only some of the game skills necessary to play the game. We called these game skills, parts of which Alucard has and parts of which I have and which become a coherent system only when they get combined, "gaming expertise". Thus, we said that the double blend Alucard-Jim is really the triple blend: Alucard ← gaming expertise → Jim.

In a game like *Full Spectrum Warrior*, this triple blend differs because "gaming expertise", while still required, is overlaid with a more distinctive expertise, namely military expertise. Here, too, the virtual character (the soldiers) and the real-world player each have different bits and pieces of knowledge and skills that need to be put together to form a coherent whole. But this coherent whole is now a form of professional military expertise, not just gaming expertise. The core actor in a game like *Full Spectrum Warrior* is a triple blend of the virtual character(s) (the soldiers), the real-world player, and their shared professional expertise: Soldiers ←gaming/military expertise → Jim. I use the formulation "gaming/military expertise" to note that in *Full Spectrum Warrior* the virtual character(s) and the real-world player share both gaming expertise (as in *Castlevania*) and military expertise, which are, of course, combined and integrated.

AUTHENTIC PROFESSIONALS

I have used words like "professional" and "expert", words that make me, and probably a good many of my readers, uneasy. The word "professional" brings to mind doctors and lawyers and other sorts of people with high status who get paid well for specialist skills. But that is not what I want to mean by the word.

What I want to mean by the word "professional" is what I will now call "authentic professionals" (what we could also call "real pros"). Authentic professionals have special knowledge and distinctive values tied to specific skills gained through a good deal of effort and experience. They do what they do, not just for money, but as a way of life. They do what they do because they are committed to an identity in which their skills and the knowledge that generates them are seen as valuable and significant. They don't operate just by well-practiced routines; they can think for themselves and innovate in their domains when they have to (Bereiter & Scardamalia 1993). Finally, authentic professionals welcome challenges at the cutting edge of their expertise.

In this sense of the word "professional", a doctor who routinely follows the dictates of the insurance company is not an authentic professional and a carpenter who has a real "attitude" about the houses he or she builds may well be. Being a professional is an identity, a state of mind, a value system built around distinctive forms of knowledge that one has earned and highly values. Being a professional is a commitment to being in the world in a certain way with a certain style and operating by certain values.

Video games like *Full Spectrum Warrior* distribute authentic professional expertise between the virtual character(s) and the real-world player. I represented this by the formula: Soldiers ← Gaming/Military Expertise → Player, arguing this blend is the core actor in the game.

Many video games involve this same sort formula, but build on different types of authentic professionalism. For example, the game *Thief: Deadly Shadows* (PC and *Xbox)* involves the professional identity of a master thief. Thieving expertise is distributed among the virtual character (Garrett) and the real-world player. So we get a formula like: Garrett ← Thieving Expertise → Player (from now on I will dispense with the formulation "gaming/thieving expertise", taking it as assumed that any distributed professional expertise built into a game is accompanied by distributed gaming expertise, as well).

The booklet for *Thief: Deadly Shadows* has this to say about you, the player, and Garrett:

> In *Thief: Deadly Shadows*, you play Garrett, a master thief in a dark, sprawling metropolis known only as the City. Rarely seen and never

caught, Garrett works alone in the shadow of night, constantly trolling for information and eyeing his next prize. He can sneak past any guard, pick any lock with ease, and infiltrate the most ingeniously secured residences. (p. 4)

Actually, of course, Garrett cannot do any of these things by himself. He has only part of the requisite knowledge and skills. He can make himself virtually disappear in the dark, blending into the background so thoroughly guards don't see him, even as they walk right past him. But you, the player, must know where and when to hide him and when to emerge from the shadows to strike. Garrett and you share a system of professional knowledge, strategies, and skills, as well as certain values (e.g., both you and Garrett need, in the game, to see artful theft as a value).

Thief has an opening tutorial in which the player is shown how to move and think like a thief by following arrows drawn on the floor and hearing words that tell you exactly what to do. In this exercise, of course, you do not feel like a professional or an expert. However, later in the game, when you have achieved more mastery, and you quietly sneak up behind some guard and knock him out, only to retreat quickly into the shadows before another guard can find you, you feel an exhilarating sense of professional mastery, an exhilarating sense of having coolly used special knowledge and skills amidst risk and danger.

If you play *Thief* in third-person view, you can watch Garrett push himself into a wall and evaporate in the shadows while a guard storms right by him. You feel a sense of power, a unique sense of embodied power as your surrogate body (Garrett's body) is both visible and on the verge of disappearing, is unseen, yet still powerfully and menacingly present. If you play in first-person view, you gain another perspective on this same power— no body is now visible on the screen, but yet you can feel yourself hiding, watching, holding yourself motionless in suspense. Either way, we see quite clearly the total blend of Garrett as virtual character, myself as player, and a shared system of knowledge, skills, values, and identity.

Garrett-Jim is, in the sense I want to use the word, an authentic professional. The point of Garrett-Jim's being is to move unseen, not to get caught, to go where others can't and steal what cannot be stolen. Garrett can't do it alone, Jim can't either. Together, sharing different aspects of a single professional tool kit, they can.

There need be no name for the profession that the virtual character and the player share. In the game *The Chronicles of Riddick: Escape from Butcher Bay*, you play Riddick. Here is what the game's booklet has to say:

> Welcome to Butcher Bay, the toughest triple-max security prison in the universe. Impossible to escape, or so they say. Inside these walls are dank tunnels, dimly lit corridors, and other hazardous areas filled with guards, savage inmates and deadly creatures that prowl the darkness. Chaos, madness, and death lurk around every corner.
>
> Only the cunning will survive. Use your strength to overpower enemies. Use your ability to see through darkness to save you. You are Richard B. Riddick, and only you can break out of this hell. (p. 2)

Riddick has special sight that allows him to see clearly even in the darkest corridor. He is so tough in words and demeanor that he inspires fear in the toughest characters (even a guard in a full robotic mech-suit calls for back up when he confronts Riddick). He can engage in great feats of athleticism in quickly moving around the vents and corridors of the prison. And, like Garrett, he can hide in shadows and attack from the dark. He exemplifies and exudes "attitude". But, you, the player, must supply the specialist tactics and strategies to instantiate Riddick's skills and values, you and Riddick must combine your skills to pull off being a professional hard-ass prison escapee of a quite distinctive sort.

There is no danger Riddick will simply follow orders—and he isn't paid in any case. He does what he does because his very special knowledge, skills, attitudes, and values have become his core identity, an identity that the player blends with to play the game.

So we not talking about professionals in the doctor-lawyer sense—many of whom aren't professionals in the sense in which I mean the term here. We are taking about authentic professionals, people who are good at something special in ways that have become part and parcel of who they are—of their identity or form of life—and in ways that allow them to innovate and navigate risk and failure. The soldiers in *Full Spectrum Warrior*, Garrett in *Thief: Deadly Shadows*, and Riddick in *The Chronicles of Riddick: Escape from Butcher Bay* are all such people. Or, really, they aren't: They are only such people when they blend with you and you add your knowledge to theirs.

You would not want to make a game in which the set of knowledge and skills shared by the virtual character and the player were not connected to some authentic professional identity. Why? Because, in that case, the game would involve the virtual character engaging only in rule-following and routine actions over and over again. No strategy or innovation would be necessary. While the player could push buttons to get the virtual character to do this, it would be just as easy to give the virtual character all the knowledge (just program in the routines) and let the player watch the game like a movie.

Even if the player was left to operate the character, the action would soon be boring and repetitive. There would soon be no challenge to the player's mind.

To be Garrett requires thought, strategy, decisions, and values. *Thief* requires these precisely because the game demands that player share an authentic professional identity and skills with a master thief. It demands more: the player must make Garrett an authentic professional thief of his or her own sort. My Garrett, for example, would not kill anyone, except in extreme cases, and loved, at times, to taunt guards by showing himself only to disappear before they could find him. Your Garrett was different.

VISION

By creating a joint authentic professional identity (in terms of knowledge, values, attitudes, practices, strategies, and skills) games like *Full Spectrum Warrior*, *Thief*, and *Riddick* also create, in the player, a new way of seeing the world. Though set in quite different locals and time periods, the physical worlds of the soldiers in *Full Spectrum Warrior*, Garrett in *Thief*, and Riddick in *Riddick* are, at a general level, pretty much the same. Like the real world they are composed of buildings and spaces. But the virtual character-player blend that each game creates demands that each of these worlds be looked at in very different ways.

Full Spectrum Warrior requires that you (the Soldiers-you) see the world as routes between cover (e.g., corners, cars, objects, walls, etc.) that will keep you protected from enemy fire. *Thief* requires that you (Garrett-you) see the world in terms of light and dark, in terms of places where you are exposed to view and places where you are hidden from view. *Riddick* requires that you (Riddick-you) see the world also in terms of light and dark (where you can hide and where you can't), though much less so than *Thief*, but also in terms of spaces where you have room for maneuver in all out physical attacks on your enemies (e.g., you don't want to get backed into a corner).

It is important—and this is something we know from recent research on the mind—that seeing and action are deeply connected for human beings (Barsalou 1999a, b; Glenberg 1997; Glenberg & Robertson 1999). Humans, when they are thinking and operating at their best, see the world in terms of affordances for actions they want to take. Thus, we see the world differently as we change our needs and desires for action. You see the world in *Full Spectrum Warrior* as routes between cover because this prepares you for the actions you need to take, namely attacking without being vulnerable to attack yourself. You see the world of *Thief* in terms of light and dark, illumination and shadows, because this prepares you for the different actions you need to take in this world, namely hiding, sneaking, appearing at just the right moment for a surprise attack, and moving unseen to your goal. So, too, with *Riddick*.

In a good game, there is a near perfect match between the virtual character's body and embodied skills, your skills as a player, the way the virtual world is perceived, and the desires, goals, and actions you share with the virtual character. This is, in fact, what a good interface in a game like the ones we are discussing is all about. Garrett (and the control system by which he is manipulated) is perfectly made to act in the world of *Thief*, if the player sees that world in the right way and has the game skills to enact this vision. From this match comes effective joint action, Garrett-Jim action.

If a player perversely insisted on seeing Garrett's world in the way in which players need to see the world of a first-person shooter like *Max Payne*, for example, Garrett would look and feel like an inept and clumsy character. He can run out and directly assault guards with his dagger, but since he can't fly smoothly through the air in slow motion while firing a clip of ammo, as May Payne can, he is usually cut down quickly. Playing the game this way is a mismatch between Garrett's body (my surrogate body in the game) and the ways in which I need to see the game's world in preparation for effective, rather than ineffective, action.

This sort of mismatch between body and world is all too common for us humans in the real world. We don't always feel a perfect match between the world, as we see it, and our body, needs, desires, and actions. When I was a kid playing soccer I could never play well or really enjoy playing because I couldn't see what was happening on the field as affordances for getting the ball to other team mates. I saw it, rather, as affordances for avoiding getting kicked in the shins by people wearing cleats. This is not a good way to see a soccer field if your action goal is, as it should be, to play the game well. For some reason I didn't have this type of problem in (American) football, where I could readily see what was happening on the field as opportunities for blocking other people (I was a center).

The same thing happens in less physical encounters. We know, for example, let us say, that we really should see what is going on, in talk and interaction, in a committee meeting as opportunities for compromise, negotiation, and reconciliation, but, nonetheless, we can't help ourselves and we see it, rather, as opportunities for attack and gaining advantage over others when they display weakness. In the end, we get thrown off the committee and the committee enacts just the sorts of policies we like least. Our way of seeing fit us for actions that weren't effective—there was a more efficacious way to see what was going on, a way that would have led to more efficacious actions in this particular setting. We were playing *Max Payne* in a *Thief* world.

When we do sense such a match between our way of seeing the world, at a particular time and place, and our action goals, and have the skills to carry these actions out, then we feel great power and satisfaction. Things click, the world looks like it was made for us. Unfortunately, this happens, for many people, more often in video games than it does in life.

KNOWING

Above I said that seeing and action are tightly connected for human beings. But so are seeing and knowing—and this, too, is a claim that is strongly supported by current research on the mind (Barsalou 1999a, b; Gee 2004; Glenberg 1997; Glenberg & Robertson 1999). Take a fact—any fact—let's say the fact that "George Washington was the first President of the United States". This fact, like all facts, is perfectly meaningless and insignificant unless and until you know what it might imply for a specific way of seeing the world. Otherwise, you really don't know anything by being able to recite this fact.

Let's say you know that some people wanted to make George Washington not the first President, but a king, so that the United States would be a monarchy as England was. George Washington, however, was opposed to this because he viewed monarchies as a reflection of the corruption, traditionalism, and lack of freedom and innovation in Europe. Now you can imagine in your mind's eye a world where the United States has a king— perhaps, George Washington with a crown amidst an aristocratic court—and juxtapose this to a vision of the way you believe the actual world was, George Washington in civilian clothes bickering with legislators. These imaginings and visions—really just perceptually-based simulations in your mind—are what give meaning to a fact like "George Washington was the first President of the United States".

To know something is to be able to imagine—to see in the theater of one's mind—what difference this makes to what the world might otherwise have looked like. Much of what we imagine, of course, stems from what we have actually seen and experienced in the real world and in texts and other media. But we can edit and combine our former seeings and experiencings into all sorts of possible worlds in our minds, each of which is a way of making sense of various facts, claims, actions, and theories.

So seeing, action, and knowing are all intimately connected. We see the world in terms of how we need and want to act on it. And how we see it, or transform our perception of it, is the foundation of meaning and significance for any and all claims to know. Video games, like *Full Spectrum Warrior*, are, at heart, blends of distinctive ways of seeing the world, acting in and on it, and knowing that world. In them eye, body, and mind become one, ironically, by blending three things: myself, the virtual character, and a distinctive authentic professional identity. That identity, we have seen, is a distinctive way of seeing, knowing, acting in, and valuing the world.

CHAPTER FIVE

FULL SPECTRUM WARRIOR AND LEARNING

If we took *Full Spectrum Warrior* as a model for learning, it would violate what both conservatives and liberals think about learning, especially learning in school. It forces the player (learner) to accept (for this time and place) a strong set of values connected to a very specific identity. Indeed, the player must follow military "doctrine" as formulated by the U. S. Army or find some other game to play. This is too constraining for the liberals.

On the other hand, *Full Spectrum Warrior* isn't about facts. There's no textbook on army doctrine. It doesn't teach by skill-and-drill. After the tutorial, which is pretty didactic, there is little explicit instruction. Rather, the player (learner) is immersed in a world of action and learns through experience, though this experience is guided or scaffolded by information the player is given and the very design of the game itself. Too much freedom here for conservative educators.

As a model of learning, *Full Spectrum Warrior* suggests that freedom requires constraints and that deep thinking requires a framework. Once the player adopts the strong values and identity the game requires, these serve as a perspective and resource from which to make decisions about actions and with which to think and resolve problems. If there is no such perspective, then there is really no basis for making any decision; no decision is really any better than any other. If there is no such perspective, then nothing I think counts as knowledge, because there is no framework within which any thought counts as any better than any other.

It is clear that if someone built a war game incorporating quite different doctrine—that is, requiring quite different values and identity—than *Full Spectrum Warrior*, then decisions and ideas that were right in that game might well be wrong in the other. For example, a doctrine that allowed soldiers to run and shoot at the same time, would lead to different sorts of decisions and different ways of solving problems in some contexts. Of course, the test of which doctrine was better in a given situation would be which one works best in that particular war setting. It is also clear that the absence of any doctrine would leave the player with no basis on which to make decisions, no basis on which to construct knowledge.

It is clear, then, that in *Full Spectrum Warrior*, its doctrine—its values and the identity it enforces on the player—is the foundation of the set of actions, decisions, and problem solutions from which the player can choose. Actions, decisions, or problem solutions outside this set are either not allowed by the game or are very unlikely to work. Of course, if there is no such set to choose from—if anything goes—then the learner has no basis on which to choose, is simply left to an infinity of choices with no good way to tell them apart.

Some liberal education does just this to children. They are immersed in rich activities—for example doing or talking about science—but with no guidance as to what are good choices, decisions, or problem solutions. The idea is, perhaps, that they will learn by making mistakes, but with so many choices available and so little basis for telling them apart, it is more likely they will go down (however creative) garden paths, wasting their time.

Let me give one concrete example of what I am talking about. Galileo discovered the laws of the pendulum because he knew and applied geometry to the problem—not because he monkeyed around with pendulums or saw a church chandelier swinging as myth has it (Matthews 1994). Yet it is common for liberal educators to ask children innocent of geometry or any other such tool to play around with pendulums and discover for themselves the laws by which they work. This is actually a harder problem than the one Galileo confronted—geometry set possible solutions for him and lead him to think about pendulums in certain ways and not others. For the children every possibility is still open and they have no powerful tools that help them approach the problem in more rather than less fruitful ways.

On the other hand, unlike conservative educators, *Full Spectrum Warrior* knows that knowledge—when one is going to engage in something like warfare—is not constituted by how many facts one can recite or how many multiple choice questions one can answer on a standardized test. No, *Full Spectrum Warrior* realizes that true knowledge in a domain (like warfare) is based on one's ability to build simulations ("models") in one's head, based on previous experiences and thoughtful conjecture, that prepare one for future action. It is also based on being able to apply values to determine whether the simulation is a good one and to evaluate its outcome when one has acted on it—values given by the values and identity with which the learner started.

One can have a purely verbal definition of a concept like "work" in physics or "bounding" in military practice. These verbal definitions are pretty useless (other than for passing tests), since they don't help facilitate future action in the domains (Gee 2004). On the other hand, if you can run a simulation in your head of how the word "work" applies to an actual type of situation in such a way that the simulation helps you prepare for action and dialogue in physics, then you really know what the concept means. The same goes for "bounding" in the military domain. Of course, you will run somewhat different simulations for "work" in different contexts and when preparing for different sorts of actions in physics. And, of course, the simulations you build will be partly determined by the wealth of experience you have had in doing and talking about physics.

If liberals often leave children too much to their own devices, conservatives often forestall their opportunities for learning to build good simulations to prepare themselves for fruitful action in a domain (like physics) by immersing them in facts, information, and tests detached from any meaningful contexts of action. Ironically, facts come free if we start from carefully guided experience (as in *Full Spectrum Warrior*) that helps learners build fruitful simulations to prepare for action. Anyone who plays *Full Spectrum Warrior* will end up knowing lots of military facts because these facts become necessary tools for building simulations and carrying out actions that the player wants and needs to carry out. The same facts become much harder to learn when detached from such simulations and actions.

Since fruitful thinking involves building simulations in our heads that prepare us for action, thinking is itself somewhat like a video game, given that video games are external simulations. If I have to meet with the boss over a problem, I can prepare myself by imagining (simulating in my mind) possible ways the meeting might go, possible responses and actions on my part, and possible outcomes. I can use such simulations—based, in part, on my earlier experiences in person or through media and, in part, on my own conjectures and imagination—to get ready for action. In action, I evaluate the outcome of my actions and run new simulations to correct for errors or mishaps.

Full Spectrum Warrior allows players to experience in a visual and embodied way military situations. They can then learn to build simulations of these in their heads and think about possible actions and outcomes before rushing into action. They can then act in the game, judge the consequences (partly based on the values and identity that military doctrine has given them), and build new, perhaps better, simulations to prepare for better actions. Without doubt the same process would work for learning in other domains, domains, say, such as biology, physics, or social science, the sorts of things we learn in school.

The recipe is simple: Give people well designed visual and embodied experiences of a domain, through simulations or in reality (or both). Help them use these experiences to build simulations in their heads through which they can think about and imaginatively test out future actions and hypotheses. Let them act and experience consequences, but in a protected way when they are learners. Then help them to evaluate their actions and the consequences of their actions (based on the values and identities they have adopted as participants in the domain) in ways that lead them to build better simulations for better future action. Though this could be a recipe for teaching science in a deep way, it is, in *Full Spectrum Warrior*, a recipe for an engaging and fun game. It should be the same in school.

Full Spectrum Warrior also realizes, as we have already seen, that deep learning—real learning—is too hard to do all by oneself. The learner needs powerful tools, like Galileo's geometry. These tools have to incorporate their own skills, knowledge, and perspectives: all of which geometry has with a vengeance—algebra works quite differently, with different in-built skills, knowledge, and perspectives, better than geometry for some things and not others.

We have seen that soldiers in *Full Spectrum Warrior* are smart, they know things. They know different things than the player, things the player doesn't have to know. This lowers the player's learning load. Furthermore, as the player gains knowledge, this knowledge can be integrated with the soldiers' knowledge to create a bigger and more powerful type of knowledge. This allows the player (learner) to do and be much more than he or she could if left all alone to his or her own devices. The actor in *Full Spectrum Warrior* is an integration of the soldiers' knowledge and the player' knowledge. The soldiers are smart tools and knowledge is distributed between them and the player.

But tools aren't any good if they do not fit with the purposes and perspectives of the learner. In *Full Spectrum Warrior* the soldiers not only know important things, they are built to fully share the doctrine—values and identity—by which the player is acting. All tools are value-laden in this way, and *Full Spectrum Warrior*'s soldiers are built with the right values, they fit with the player's emerging intentions built on the player's emerging values and identity (based on the doctrine the game enforces).

Full Spectrum Warrior allows players to integrate their emerging professional military knowledge with the professional knowledge of the soldiers. The player, in this way, is guided into thinking, acting, valuing, and deciding like a professional of a certain sort. The player experiences the feel of expertise even before the player is a real expert or even really expert at the game. This is a beautiful example of an important learning principle virtually ignored in school: performance before competence.

Schools usually insist that learners study hard, become competent (the test shows it!), and then perform (and, yet, research shows they usually can't actually do anything beyond answer test questions). Of course, there is little motivation to study and become competent, when the learner has no real idea what it feels like to act effectively in a domain or why anyone would want to become competent in the area. Further, all the facts and information the learners is studying would make a lot more sense if the learner had had any opportunities to see how they applied to the world of action and experience. Without that, they are "just words" for the learner.

In *Full Spectrum Warrior*, on the other hand, the player (learner) performs, even when not very competent, aided by the soldier's knowledge, the doctrine the game is enforcing, and the very design of the game world itself. Players feel competent before they are. They know what it means to be competent and why anyone would want to be competent in the domain. They pick up facts, information, skills, tricks of the trade. They enact values and a certain identity. All of sudden—miracles of miracles—they are competent. And, further, they are competent in a sense well beyond just being able to answer test questions. They can act, value, feel, decide, and solve problems like a pro or at least like a novice pro, a pro in the making now. Maybe they will never become a real professional, but they will always know what it was like to act and feel like one in that area.

Learning school things, things like biology, say, could work in just the same way. Strong doctrine, values and identity, smart tools, distributed knowledge, well designed experience, guidance on how to build useful mental models or simulations and on how to evaluate their outcomes, performance before competence, competence that goes beyond verbal definitions and test taking (Shaffer 2004). But, in reality, this is all very rare, indeed, in school, though common in good video games.

Of course, I know that some readers are put off by my military example and still quite disturbed by that strong term "doctrine". Strong doctrine, leading to values and identity, engagement and commitment, real choices from within a reasonable and fruitful set of choices, and ways to evaluate what one has done are necessary for real learning, however much they comport badly with the beliefs of liberal educators. It is a pity, indeed, that we have such good examples of such good learning in the military domain, both in the case of commercial games like *Full Spectrum Warrior* and non-commercial simulations used by the military for training, and not in domains like biology, physics, history, social science, urban planning, ecology, and many other more academic-like domains. It is equally a pity that the military does not have simulations as good as the ones they have for warfare for understanding culture and building peace (or running prisons).

But there is no reason in principle why this should be so. It surely is a shame that we live in a society that adopts a deeper theory of learning in its video games and in its training of soldiers than it does in its schools. It is surely also a shame that the military so often succeeds with the very 18-year-olds that the schools have failed with. Whatever one thinks of modern technological warfare in a global world (I don't like it), it is not something that dummies can do.

But, of course, strong doctrine, values, and identity can lead to intolerant ideologues, as well, whether these be soldiers, scientists, or religious fanatics. There is a paradox here, of course: no deep learning without doctrine and doctrine can be dangerous. But this paradox is easy to resolve at the educational level: Be sure that learners have lived and acted in multiple worlds based on different doctrines. Be sure they can compare and contrast and think about the relationships among doctrines. They'll make smart choices, then, I believe, about what ultimately to believe and how ultimately to act.

Some doctrines work better than others for given situations and learners will learn this. Here, again, the video game industry is out ahead: the store shelves are full of different worlds based on different doctrines. *Full Spectrum Warrior* sits alongside *Thief* and *Riddick*. Maybe someday it will sit beside Galileo's world and doctrines, as well.

Rise of Nations

CHAPTER SIX

RISE OF NATIONS

Strategy and Identity

In the Chapter 3 we developed the formula:

Virtual Character ← Authentic Professional Expertise → Player

and discussed how this formula worked out in different games:

Full Spectrum Warrior:
Soldiers ← Professional Military Expertise → Player

Thief: Deadly Shadows:
Garrett ← Professional Thief → Player

The Chronicles of Riddick: Escape from Butcher Bay:
Riddick ← Professional Hard-Ass Escapee → Player

Of course, the shared professional expertise found in a video game does not have to be authentic in a real world sense. I have no idea whether Garrett's skills and knowledge closely follow those of real master thieves or not. It doesn't matter. All that matters is that he and I behave like authentic professionals in that we leverage special skills and knowledge as part and parcel of a certain value system and identity. We feel like experts to ourselves and revel in our expertise.

When games like those we have been discussing create a shared authentic professional expertise between the virtual character(s) and the player, they open up play to two crucial variables: strategy and identity. We will discuss strategy in this chapter and identity in the Chapter 8, though I will quickly say something about both now, before turning to a more detailed discussion of strategy games in this chapter.

As I pointed out in Chapter 2, a game like *Castlevania* requires generic gaming skills. It also requires strategy, but, again, strategic thinking of a generic gaming sort. The player must think of good strategic uses of the virtual character's movements and attacks within the configuration of the game space. But the games above require—and all allow for a range of—strategies rooted in the professional skills the player shares with the virtual character(s), whether these be military skills, thieving skills, or hard-ass prison escapee skills.

The strategies a player puts into play in a game like *Full Spectrum Warrior* come to constitute an intricate and slow dance of movements from cover to cover, all in pursuit of the most advantageous positioning against the enemy's positions. Players use the built-in GPD device, the experience they have already gotten from previous play, and their skills at reading the physical environment in a military way in the service of carrying out a strategy that unfolds over time. At all times they must follow military "doctrine", that is, the rules of professional military engagement as these are seen by the U.S. Army. The thinking required in *Thief* is quite different, and different again in *Riddick*.

But adding authentic professionalism to a game does not just open up a unique space for strategy, it also opens up a unique space for identity. An authentic professional has values and attitudes, as well as characteristic ways of talking, acting, and interacting, connected to his or skill special skills and knowledge. These values, attitudes, and ways of talking, acting, and interacting constitute an identity. In blending with the virtual character—in acting out of a shared set of skills—the player takes on this identity. The player gets to play with, think about, and empathize with this identity in an embodied way, since the virtual character is the player's surrogate body in the game world.

Each soldier in *Full Spectrum Warrior* has an identity very different than Riddick's. They never rush into open battle, they are not loners, they don't taunt their enemies. Garrett has a different identity from either the *Full Spectrum Warrior* soldiers or Riddick. Here is what the booklet that comes with *Thief* has to say about Garrett:

> Cynical and unenthusiastic about helping those in need, Garrett draws on his talents to life from the wealthy solely for his own gain. To him, everyone is a potential victim who can help line his pockets and fuel the underground economy of the City. He's a legend among his own kind, a reluctant anti-hero who wants nothing more than to be left alone to carry out his trade. But instead his actions seem to always draw him into greater conflicts. (p. 4)

However, this is not quite right—but, wait a minute, how can I say this is not right? How can I know better than the game's designers who Garrett is? Because I was Garrett.

My Garrett (Garrett-Jim) would not kill anyone unless it was necessary. At one point in the game, frustrated by my inability to sneak by or knock out a particular guard, I killed him from the shadows with a well shot arrow. This made me (Jim) feel bad, because this was not the sort of person I wanted Garrett (really Garrett-Jim) to be. I reloaded the game from the last save, and eventually got past the guard without killing him.

My Garrett did not steal primarily to "line his pockets". While I fenced my stolen goods to pay for essentials, I spent very little of the money I obtained from what I had stolen. My Garrett (Garrett-Jim) stole primarily as an artistic achievement. My Garrett got his deepest pleasure when he emptied a rich museum that had proudly boasted in the newspaper that it was thief-proof. He (I) took his (my) deed as a statement about the rich and their pretensions.

So my Garrett—Garrett-Jim—is not the designers' Garrett, not exactly the one they wrote about in their booklet. Just as Garrett and I share a distributed skill set (the distributed knowledge and skills of an authentic professional thief shared out between us), we also share an identity. He has part of it—he talks, acts, interacts, and values in certain ways set by the designers—but I have part of it as well. I determine some of his actions (e.g., not needlessly killing a guard) and, most importantly, I supply his emotions and some of his values. I feel for him.

I cannot be any sort of Garrett I want. The parameters of his identity are set by the game's designers. But within those parameters, there is space for many Garretts, one of whom is (was) Garrett-Jim.

Supplying emotions, values, and value-laden decisions, as well as strategic thinking, to a virtual character, within the parameters set by the character's (share of) authentic professional skills and identity is a heady experience. I gain a new body, a new mind, a new life, without losing my own.

When I played *Riddick*, my emotions, values, and value-laden decisions, as well as my strategies, were far different than they had been in *Thief*. Though Riddick, too, can sneak by enemies without killing them, Riddick-Jim killed any and all of them. I restarted *Riddick* not when I failed to kill someone, but when I had done it so sloppily and poorly that I felt it made Riddick's tough-guy character look bad.

At one point in *Riddick*, Riddick needs to get out of one part of a prison he is in so he can move to another part where he will be better able to escape. There are two ways he can do this. He can either kill a series of inmate opponents in fighting matches on which others have placed bets or he can do favors for a drug addict who will then give him drugs. In either case, he uses these events to get himself brought to the prison's warden (in the last fight of the series, he kills an inmate favored by the jail's warden; in the drug case, he allows himself to get caught with the drugs, which are contraband). When confronted with the warden and his henchmen, Riddick kills them all, and enters parts of the prison from which he can eventually escape for good.

Initially, I couldn't win the last fight in the series of matches, because I had allowed myself to get too low on health in the previous fights. So I went the drug route. However, I then felt that this just wasn't Riddick; Riddick would and should have won the fights handily. So I restarted the game from a save before the whole series of fights and won the fights, avoiding the drug route.

So Riddick-Jim was not Garrett-Jim, not just because Riddick is not Garrett, but because Jim is not always the same Jim. Games are an invitation to play out different sides of our desires, feelings, values, fears, fantasies, and identities. Riddick recruited a different Jim than Garrett did.

So adding authentic professionalism to games adds strategy (beyond gaming strategy itself) and identity. It is pretty clear these are not really completely separate things. The values I take on help determine the decisions I will make and thus the range of strategies I will contemplate. Strategies that I played out in *Riddick* were not open to me in *Thief,* even when the game allowed them, because my values and decisions—my identity—was different in that game.

This opening up of strategy and identity via authentic professionalism is also the space where two very different types of video games can arise. These two are quite different from each other and quite different, again, from games like *Full Spectrum Warrior, Thief,* and *The Chronicle of Riddick: Escape from Butcher Bay.* They are strategy games (like *Rise of Nations*), on the one hand, games that extend the strategy side that authentic professionalism opens up, and role playing games (like *The Elder Scrolls III: Morrowind*), on the other hand, games that extend the identity side that authentic professionalism opens up. We will first talk about strategy and then, in the Chapter 8, about identity.

STRATEGY GAMES

In *Full Spectrum Warrior,* the player controls two squads of four soldiers each. These soldiers move and shoot under the player's orders, but the player does not him or herself directly control or fire any weapon. This means that players have a different relationship to these virtual characters than they do to Garrett or Riddick, characters who they do directly manipulate.

In *Full Spectrum Warrior,* you issue an order or a series of orders and watch your squads carry them out. For example, you order Squad A to lay down suppression fire and order Squad B to move from one place to another while the enemy is engaged by Squad A's suppression fire and, thus, cannot react to Squad B's movement in a timely fashion. On the other hand, in *Thief,* you actually directly move Garrett around. You don't order him to shoot an arrow, you use his body to aim and shoot. You don't order him to sneak and attack, you use his body to sneak up behind a guard and hit the guard with a club to knock him out.

Thief allows the player to play Garrett in either third-person perspective (where you see his body) or first person perspective (where you see only the weapon he/you are carrying). If you play in first-person perspective, you feel like your body is inside the space taken up by Garrett's body, though you see nothing (but a weapon or hands) in this space. If you play in third-person perspective, you feel doubled. When Garrett moves, you feel both as if you are looking over Garrett's shoulder and as if you are moving along with him.

First-person mode feels closer to the character and allows you to identify tightly with Garrett's situatedness in the world. Third-person mode allows you to see Garrett's body, actions, and reactions and identify with him from a thematic point of view, since you now have images to help with the identity play you are engaged in in being Garrett.

In *Full Spectrum Warrior*, your point of views (perspective) feels outside and a bit above the eight soldiers you command. You identify with any one of them less than you do with Garrett or Riddick, though in the game they each do have separate personalities. You identify with them less because there are many of them, not just one, and because you don't control them directly, but as teams to whom you give orders.

We can imagine how *Full Spectrum Warrior* works being carried further and further. What if you commanded not just eight soldiers, but a hundred? What about a whole division? What about a division and all its tanks, artillery, and vehicles? What if you commanded an army, a navy, and an air force, including soldiers, vehicles, and planes? What if you not only commanded soldiers, but also gave commands to have buildings built, units trained, scientific research carried out, taxes and resources collected, and international negotiations carried out?

Of course, such games exist—they are called strategy games, like the classic *Civilization* series, and, if the player operates in real-time (i.e., while the player is doing things, his or her opponents are also, at the same time, doing things, so it matters who operates faster), they are called real-time strategy games, games like *Rise of Nations*, *Age of Mythology*, and *WarCraft*. In such games, players build and command whole civilizations, building them up from "primitive" stages to more and more advanced stages by collecting resources, building buildings, settling new land and building whole new cities, engaging in research, fighting wars, and engaging in diplomacy.

At each stage, moving up from *Full Spectrum Warrior*'s eight soldiers to commanding and building a whole civilization, the player moves away from the perspective of any one character and higher up above the whole scene, looking down on it as a god-like being. Indeed, *Full Spectrum Warrior* is just the first step in this sort of progression. It is part way between an action-adventure game like *Thief* or *Riddick* and a strategy game like *Rise of Nations*.

What this movement out and up to god status does is accomplish three things. First, it lessens the identification with a virtual character or characters. Second, it makes the virtual characters the player manipulates (and this now includes groups, large and small, buildings, fleets, and resources) less like individuals and more like tools or resources for carrying out complicated tasks. And, third, it creates a space in which the player concentrates primarily on using these tools to create and carry out strategies and strategic plans, that is, a long string of connected and coherent strategies operating over a long period of time and over a large amount of space.

Because the lessening of personal identification can sometimes make these sorts of games feel a bit "cold" and "calculating", compared to the up close and personal identification one has with Garrett or Riddick, some of them allow players to have heroes with special powers, characters that stick out from the crowd (as in *WarCraft III* or *Age of Mythology*, see especially the *Titians* expansion).

The god perspective of these games plays up the strategy element to its fullest. The player feels like a god who uses people, groups, objects, time, and space as tools or resources to carry out both small and grand strategies in competition with other civilizations run by other gods (either other real players in multi-player games or the computer operating as if it were another real player).

This creates an entirely different type of game. We have pretty much moved as far from *Castlevania*, in one direction (there is another), as we can. We argued in Chapter 2 that in a game like *Castlevania*, there are two stories. One is the designer's story (a story about a family that fights vampires through the ages). We argued that this is not the primary story in a game like *Castlevania*. The primary story is the second story: This second story is the unique trajectory that Alucard and I—Alucard-Jim—have taken through the game. This second story—the important story in playing *Castlevania*—is the Alucard-Jim story, the virtual-real story. It is the record of the order and manner in which Alucard-Jim went places in the game, did deeds in the game, and solved problems in the game. This record is different for each player.

In Chapter 4, we argued that there are three stories in a game like *Full Spectrum Warrior*. *Full Spectrum Warrior* adds a third story, what we called a career, to the sort of second story (a trajectory) and first story (the designers' story) that games like *Castlevania* have.

In *Full Spectrum Warrior*, there is a designers' story (about terrorists in Zekastan) and this, again, is not the primary story from a game playing perspective. As in *Castlevania*, there is a second story in *Full Spectrum Warrior*, a story that is more important. This is the trajectory through the game each player takes, a trajectory that is different for each player. Each player has taken different routes through the game and been places and done things in a different order.

The third story in a game like *Full Spectrum Warrior*, we argued, comes about because, in such a game, the second story, the trajectory, transmutes into a quite different type of story. The story now—this third story—goes beyond just where I've been and when I've done what I've done in the game (*Castlevania*'s second story). This third story is the story of the soldiers and Jim's enactment of professional knowledge. In *Castlevania*, Alucard and Jim share no professional knowledge or practice. But in *Full Spectrum Warrior*, the soldiers (virtual characters) and Jim do share such knowledge and practice. They have distributed knowledge of military values, strategies, practices, and skills. This fact gives rise to the third story.

This third story is the story of *our career* (the soldiers and me) as military professionals. Each player has made different strategic military choices, engaged in different military tactics, enacted military values in different places and different ways, succeeded and failed at different places and tasks with military significance. Once again, these choices have been enacted by the player blended with the virtual characters, the soldiers—a blend that is fully necessary here, since military knowledge is distributed between these two.

The second story here (a player's trajectory through the game in terms of the order in which they gone places and done things) and the third story (the soldiers and my career in terms of the progressive joint deployment of professional military knowledge), as we said earlier, blend together, of course and are only usefully distinguished for analytical purposes.

Strategy games like *Rise of Nations* add a fourth story to the designers' story (the first story), the virtual character-player's unique trajectory through the game (the second story), and the virtual character-player's career (the third story). This fourth story is a *history* in a sense of the word I will explicate after a few brief remarks about the game itself.

Real-time strategy games like *Rise of Nations* are among the most complex and demanding of computer and video games. In such games, players play a civilization of their choosing, a civilization for which they must make a myriad of decisions. They send their citizens out to gather resources (e.g., food, wood, minerals, gold, etc.) and use these resources to build domestic and military buildings and engage in various forms of research. In these buildings, they can train soldiers and other sorts of people (e.g., leaders, priests, scientists, or professors), as well as build military and other sorts of apparatus. As they gather and build, they can advance to different ages, allowing their civilization to achieve higher levels of complexity and sophistication. All the while they must go to war against, or engage in diplomacy with, other civilizations.

All of this is done in real time. While the player builds up his or her civilization, other players (or the computer representing other players) are building up theirs as well. Players must decide when to attack or engage in diplomacy. Victory may come to the swift, that is, to those who attack early (a strategy called "rushing"), or to those who wait and patiently build up (a strategy called "turtling").

Rise of Nations (along with its expansion *Rise of Nations: Thrones and Patriots*) is one of the best real-time strategy games ever made (along with such excellent games as *StarCraft, WarCraft III: Reign of Chaos*, and *Age of Mythology*). *Rise of Nations*, in its expansion pack version, allows the player to play one of 24 civilizations (e.g., Aztecs, Bantu, British, Chinese, Egyptians, Maya, Nubians, Russians, Spanish, etc.), each with different advantages and disadvantages. The player can play against one to seven opponents (other real people or the computer playing other civilizations). Players can move through eight ages from the Ancient Age to the Information Age through various intervening ages such as the Medieval Age, the Gunpowder Age, and the Enlightenment Age.

Like all real-time strategy games, *Rise of Nations* involves players learning well over a hundred different commands, each connected to decisions that need to be made, as they move through a myriad of different menus (there are 102 commands on the abridged list that comes printed on a small sheet enclosed with the original game). Furthermore, players must sometimes operate at top speed if they are to keep up with skilled opponents who are building up as they are. *Rise of Nations* involves a great deal of micromanagement and decision making under time pressure.

Rise of Nations has a designer's story, though in a very loose sense: it is about different historically-based civilizations competing with each other for land and conquest. Real-time strategy games don't need to be about real historical civilizations. *Age of Mythology* is about ancient societies and their mythological characters and gods; *StarWars: Battleship Gallectia* is about different civilizations in the Star Wars universe; *Spell Force: The Order of Dawn* is about mages, humans, dwarves, elves, and orcs.

Rise of Nations has a second story with a vengeance. It is nearly impossible for any two players to move through the game in the same way. The trajectory that each player and his or her chosen civilization take through the game is always unique. Each player-civilization pair builds things, settles new land, and triggers various events at different times and in different orders. For example, in *Rise of Nations* I may have built a large army well before my opponent, but have entered the Gunpowder Age well after that opponent (and there can be more than one opponent).

Rise of Nations has a third story, as well, a player-civilization career. In such a game, I share authentic professional skills with the myriad of virtual characters and objects I control. The professional skills here are some version of world/civilization building, including warfare skills. My peasants know how to plant farms and farm them, but I have to know when and where to tell them to do this. My archers know how to group themselves and fight, but I have to know when and where to use them and how many of them to have along with other types of troops. My university professors know how to accumulate knowledge my civilization can use, but I have to know when and where to build universities and how best to use the benefits these universities give my civilization. And so on and so forth through many other domains.

In the end, when I have finished a game play session (which can take a long time), there is a story to tell about my career as a professional world builder and world beater, just as there was a story to tell about my career as a squad commander in Full *Spectrum Warrior*. For example, in my career I may have stressed building a solid economy as a base for expansion, while you stressed quick raids by marauding war parties. I was an economics-focused world builder and you were a raiding-party world builder. I may have stressed alliances and diplomacy, you may have stressed heavy taxation for the upkeep of large armies that attacked enemies on several fronts at once.

But there is a new, fourth story to a game like *Rise of Nations*. In games like *Full Spectrum Warrior*, *Thief*, and *The Chronicles of Riddick* there is one in-game actor (Garrett, Riddick) or a very small set of them (Alpha and Bravo Squads) with which the player blends. In these games, events take place over a fairly short time period (days or weeks at most). In a game like *Rise of Nations*, there are a myriad of actors (peasants, soldiers, scholars, buildings, vehicles of all sorts, farms, oil wells, logging camps, air bases, etc.) with which the player blends, they change over time (no guns to begin with, no air bases to begin with, nuclear weapons only at the end, each building and soldier changes its look and function with each changing age), and events unfold over a long stretch of story time (ages).

All this means that there is a story here to be told not just about your career as world builder and world beater, but also a story about the *history* you are making. Events, which ultimately you controlled, unfolded over the long haul, but in such a way that at the end of the game, this history is also the story of why you won (or lost). In a game like *Rise of Nations*, you can come to see that things that you made or let happen in one age have consequences later on, maybe many ages later. Like all history, this story is not only the story of things unfolding over significant time, it is also a story of multiple actors, deeds, and objects interacting in complex ways though an extended period of time.

History arises when I can talk about events forming patterns over long periods of time. It arises when I can segment events into meaningful different time periods. It arises when I can talk about significant changes and development over time and in one period as compared to another. In even one play session of *Rise of Nations*, I create, with all the actors and things in my civilization, a history, a trajectory through a long enough time that I can talk and think in terms of historical duration. Indeed, the game offers players at the end of each play session a full set of statistics about all aspects of the history and time line they have created, compared to that created by the opposing civilizations.

In a game like *Rise of Nations*, I, a mere individual human, come to embody not Garrett, or Riddick, or a few soldiers and their careers as authentic professionals, I come to embody a history of people, things, places, and times. I have left my body altogether. I have become a god, albeit sometimes a losing god, a god on the wrong side of history. Heady stuff, indeed.

How can this happen? Well part of the answer lies, as we have already said, in rising from the close-to-my-virtual-character perspective of games like *Thief* and *Riddick*, rising even beyond the close-to-my-squad perspective of *Full Spectrum Warrior*, to a god-like perspective over a whole myriad of virtual actors and objects. But the heart of the answer lies in this: in a game like *Rise of Nations* each virtual character (e.g., soldiers) and object (e.g., types of buildings) shares with the player not only world-building skills (this is the authentic professionalism shared out in these games), but also what I will call a *developmental capacity*.

Say you are playing the British in *Rise of Nations*. The small hut you build at the start of your civilization to serve as your town center will change its shape, size, and function with each passing age, becoming bigger, more modern, and more powerful. The simple foot soldier brandishing a sling and rocks in the Ancient Age will gain better weapons, protection, and skills with each passing age, eventually becoming a modern soldier. Your simple logging camps will become industrial sites, your oil wells will become huge refineries, through various stages. And so on for every actor and object in the game.

Each actor and object—for example that simple foot soldier Slinger—has a developmental capacity. The actor or object has the capacity to change, improve, and develop over the course of the game. The British Slinger in the Ancient Age will become a Javelineer in the Classical Age, an Elite Javelineer in the Medieval Age, an Arquebusier in the Gunpowder Age, a Highlander in the Enlightenment Age, a Black Watchman in the Industrial Age, a member of the Infantry in the Modern Age and part of an Assault Infantry in the Information Age.

When and where each (type of) actor and object (e.g., building, town or city, type of boat, university, etc.) changes depends on the player's decisions and strategies. The player's acts and decisions decide when each new age dawns (and everything changes). A player in a game like *Rise of Nations* needs to view each actor and object not as one thing, but really as a set of potential things, each one more developed than the last (e.g., more and more powerful and modern types of soldiers or buildings or farms, etc.).

Each actor and thing in a game like *Rise of Nations* needs to be seen as a trajectory through a developmental space. When players are building simple Slingers in the beginning stage of their civilization, if they are playing the British, for example, they need to consider when, where, and why—in strategic terms—these warriors will be transformed into Javelineers, Elite Javelineer, Arquebusiers, and so forth. The same sort of decision has to be made for every other sort of object in the game. Are my wood camps and mines sufficient for my needs or should I push to an age with oil wells, as well as more modern logging and mining?

The player's decision can come too early or too late. It can come at a time where the battle is already lost in one place, but where it turns the tide of battle in another spot on the map. Players can choose not to move on to newer ages and try to defeat their opponents quickly before these opponents have had the opportunity to advance to new, more powerful ages. Or players can wait until they have nuclear weapons in the Information Age before they seek total victory.

So, in a game like *Rise of Nations*, the player and the virtual characters (actors and objects, in this case) share not only professional skills (world building and world beating skills), but they also share a developmental capacity. The virtual actors and objects know how to change with each age, how to evolve and develop, but the player has to know when to transform them and how to best use that transformation to his or her advantage.

Thus, with games like *Rise of Nations* we get yet a new formula to add to our others. Such games do honor our earlier formula about authentic professionalism, thanks to the fact that virtual characters and the player share professional world building/world beating skills:

Virtual Character ← Authentic Professional Expertise → Player
(World Building Expertise)

But they also introduce a new formula:

Virtual Character ← Developmental Capacity → Player

It is this shared developmental capacity that gives rise to a unique history (a fourth story) in games like *Rise of Nations* for each civilization-player blend (e.g., British-Jim), just as it was the shared authentic professionalism that gave rise to a unique career for each virtual character-player blend. It is not for nothing that *Full Spectrum Warrior*'s soldiers, *Thief*'s Garrett, and *The Chronicles of Riddick*'s Riddick don't age. They have no developmental capacity. Furthermore, they don't get better and better at what they do; they don't learn new things over stretches of time, though the player usually does. They can give the player a sense of having had a career as a particular type of authentic professional but they cannot really give the player a sense of having had and made a developmental history.

Of course, a game could offer a history making capacity and still be about only one virtual character (like Garrett or Riddick). But this character would have to share a developmental capacity with the player. The virtual character would have to have the capacity to develop through a long stretch of time and this potential would need to require the player's strategic thinking as to how, where, and when this developmental capacity should unfold to change the nature and even outcome of the game.

For such a game it would not be enough that the virtual character ages, nor would the character have to show age by looking older and older. The virtual character would have to develop over time and the player would need to choose when and where (even how) the character developed and how to use these changes in the game. In this case, the virtual character and the player would together have played out a developmental capacity of a certain sort and would have given rise to a personal (individual) history, a life history.

Such games, of course, exist. I said at the outset of this chapter that when games like *Full Spectrum Warrior*, *Thief*, and *Riddick* create a shared authentic professional expertise between the virtual character(s) and the player, they open up play to two crucial variables: strategy and identity. Games like *Rise of Nations* take off further on the strategy side by rising above the virtual characters in a god-like fashion, using them as tools and resources with developmental capacities for history building. But role-playing games like *The Elder Scrolls III: Morrowind* take off further on the identity side by delving more deeply into one virtual character, giving them a developmental capacity that can be used for building a life history. In the Chapter 8 we turn to games like *Morrowind*.

But before we turn to such games, we should ask: What is the pleasure of games like *Rise of Nations*? We almost don't have to ask. Who doesn't want to be god, who doesn't want to make meaning on the scale of history? Life gives few people the opportunity to feel control over things on a large scale. *Rise of Nations* gives anyone and everyone this feeling. This feeling, this pleasure, once reserved only for kings, presidents, and the very rich, is now open to everyone.

A game like *Rise of Nations* is the very opposite of a game like *Tetris* or *Castlevania*. Here is what we said about *Tetris* in Chapter 2:

> We first confront a world where everything looks pretty much the same and pretty simple—just falling shapes with interlocking parts. It's quite clear what the rules are. But, as we play, we come to see that this sameness (simplicity) hides a great wealth of different possibilities, different problems and different solutions, a good deal of complexity. In *Tetris*, unlike "real" life, we start from simplicity and discover complexity.
>
> In *Tetris*, a set of simple rules (rules that define a set of shapes, rates of fall, and possible combinations of the shapes) generates a complex array of different problems. Simplicity gives rise to complexity in a quite obvious fashion. In life, we often find ourselves hoping (often vainly) that some set of simple rules exists that will give meaning and order to the complexity we face. In *Tetris* we see clearly that this is the case.
>
> *Tetris*, thus, models one of our deepest human desires: to solve problems by finding patterns inside a safe world in which there is a clear and comforting underlying order. We see the order (simplicity, pattern) clearly and we safely play among the surprising complexity the game generates always knowing that simplicity and order is there. This sort of event is rare in people's daily lives in the real world. *Tetris* is an escape into the very desire for order, control, and workable solutions that we have all the time in our daily lives, a desire often frustrated in life, but never in *Tetris*. We understand our successes and failures.

We argued in Chapter 2 that *Castlevania* gives rise to a similar set of pleasures as *Tetris*, but adds to these the pleasure of generating and finding patterns in terms of story elements, that is, actions, actors, events, and states. A game like *Rise of Nations* works differently. Here we start with utter difference and complexity, not simplicity and a simple set of rules that map nicely to shapes, movements, and actions. There seem to be no simple set of rules. There are a great many commands to master. There are many virtual elements (actors and objects) to control. Things happen over ages. There is nothing but complexity.

We desperately seek to tame this complexity, to find patterns over time. We seek to find history—because, in a sense, that's all history is, an attempt to tell a story that makes sense of a myriad of actors and events over time. In a game like *Rise of Nations* we find history, not by telling it, but making it, and then seeing it represented in a set of graphs and statistics at the end of the our play session.

This is a type of order, pattern, and sense making that, in the real world, it takes libraries of books to argue for and which we always suspect, in our chaotic and dangerous world, never really holds, is always open to being blown apart. Not in *Rise of Nations*. When my British Arquebusiers, Elite Pikemen, and Kings Yeomen take to the field in the Gunpowder Age I know this will all, in the end, make sense and sense on a large scale. And, better yet, it will make sense because I, like god, made it happen. Even if I lose, I know why I lost.

CHAPTER SEVEN

RISE OF NATIONS AND LEARNING

Strategy games like *Rise of Nations* are ripe with implications for new ways of thinking about learning in our modern high-tech, global world. They are ripe, too, with implications for how to build better learning in and out of schools. But before I discuss specific implications for learning that flow from such games, let me pause to discuss one aspect of learning important to all good video games. This aspect, it turns out, takes a particularly important and clear form in strategy games like *Rise of Nations*.

Video games represent a new technology with important implications. This new technology creates a potential learning environment that shares little with traditional schooling, but much with how learning, thinking, and understanding work at the cutting edge of the sciences and other professional domains.

When we play games, we gamers are cyborgs. We gain a new body part—the controller—that, like the blind person's cane, becomes an extension of our bodies, allowing us to extend our minds into a space otherwise beyond our reach. But in playing a video game we do more than enter a heretofore unreachable space.

Take any good video game as an example, say *Onimusha 3: Demon Siege*. *Demon Siege* opens with a stunning CG movie in which the samurai Hidemitsu Samanosuke Akechi single-handedly fights the monster hoard of Lord Nobunaga. It's a thrilling scene, but yet no different than a book or a movie. The scene is "out there". I am its spectator. The scene does make me say to myself: "I want to do that", "I want to be that". And, indeed, when the game starts, low and behold, I can do that and be that.

Surely such "immersion" is one of the great powers of video games. But it is not their only or main power. Nor is it what sets video games apart from books or movies. I can "lose myself" in a good book or movie as readily as I can lose myself in a good video game. The power of video games is not in losing ourselves, but in finding a new being, neither real nor virtual, a blended, fused being.

When I play *Demon Siege* I don't actually become Samanosuke Akechi. I don't mean by this remark to make the trivial point that I don't actually become Samanosuke in the real world. Of course, I don't. I mean to say, that the person living and acting in the *Demon Siege* world—the actor in the game—is not me, nor is it Samanosuke; rather, it is a third blended being whom the video game has brought into existence in and through the act of playing. It is James Hidemitsu Samanosuke Gee Akechi. Such a person exists neither in the real world nor in the virtual world that the game's designers have made. When I "lose myself" in *Demon Siege*, I also find this new being, this James Hidemitsu Samanosuke Gee Akechi. Let's call such beings "real-virtual beings".

We have, of course, spent a good deal of time already in this book discussing this sort of blended being, the virtual character and the real-world player that share gaming skills and, in some games, authentic professional skills. But, nonetheless, let's think a bit more about this blended being.

So who is James Hidemitsu Samanosuke Gee Akechi? *Demon Siege*, like any good video game of its sort, is a world in a box, but a very special kind of world. It is a world that allows the player to stretch between the real world and a virtual world. The player has a foot, body, and mind in each world. This stretching-and-acting-between-two-worlds creates a third identity which is neither real nor virtual. It is here that the true power of video games lies. It is here that a new power for learning—and not just for learning, but for social change, as well—arises.

This real-virtual being—this James Hidemitsu Samanosuke Gee Akechi—arises because the game allows me, a real person, to achieve a form of embodied movement in a virtual world, thanks to my surrogate body (Samanosuke) inside the virtual world. But it is important to realize that a game world is not just eye candy. It is, in fact, a *complex system*. This complex system is an emergent property of the (sometimes not fully understood) rules that the designer has built into the game and the (never predictable) interactions of the player (and his or her gamer identity) with this rule system.

This blended, fused being, this James Hidemitsu Samanosuke Gee, becomes a powerful *tool* with which to understand, in an embodied way, the complex system that the game represents. So what embodied movement in the game world actually means is this: I, the player, can achieve an *embodied empathy for a complex system*. That is, I identify with, at an empathetic level, not just a character, but with a *complex system*, since I am simultaneously inside and outside the system.

The world is full of complex systems—they are the things cutting-edge scientists most often study these days—things like the weather, the inside of an atom, cells, solar systems, computer networks, ecological systems, cultures and social systems, and so forth (Holland 1999; Kauffman 1995). So far in history, for most people, complex systems have not been the sorts of warm and fuzzy things with which most people could sympathize, let alone empathize. But good games create a strong empathetic identification with the game world as a system—otherwise you simply move in the beautiful world, admire it, and quickly die—try it in game like *Far Cry* and see just how long you last.

There is another place where real-virtual beings exist, another place where embodied empathy for a complex system is achieved, and that is at the cutting-edge of the hardest of hard sciences. Just as we can only understand gamers by watching them play, we can only understand scientists by watching them play (work). So let's watch some (example from Ochs, Gonzales, & Jacoby 1996, pp. 330-331). Consider the remark below from a physicist talking to a few other physicists in the field of solid state physics. Of necessity I include the physicists gestures and body movements—we're talking about embodiment here, after all:

> But as you go below the first order transition you're
> (leans upper body to right) still
> in the domain structure and you're still trying to get
> (sweeps right arm to left) out of it.
> Well you also said
> (moves to board; points to diagram) the same thing
> must happen here.
> (Points to the right side of the diagram) When
> (moves finger to left) I come down
> (moves finger to right) I'm in
> (moves finger to left) the domain state

This is professional physics talk for physicists who study things like atoms spinning inside magnetic fields. In such talk these scientists conflate, blend, fuse their real world selves (as scientific professionals) with the object of their scientific concern (in this case, atomic spin inside a magnetic field). They pull off this conflation by imaginatively moving their own bodies and minds inside a diagram which is a model of spinning atoms (and a model is a type of virtual world—by the way this diagram happens itself to be related to a computer simulation of the same phenomenon). The real and the virtual are melded to create a real-virtual being. In turn, this real-virtual being (the real "I" moving inside the virtual model of the domain state) becomes a new tool (just like James Hidemitsu Samanosuke Gee Akechi) with which to think and act, in this case, to think and act with the highest forms of understanding in this area of physics. Identity, practice, virtual world (the diagram), and real world have been utterly fused.

This type of physics involves learning a new form of *seeing* and *feeling*, a new way to see and feel from the perspective of being embodied within a complex system, while still, of course, remaining in and acting out of the real world of one's professional practice as a physicist. This is embodied empathy for a complex system with a vengeance. It is one way in which physics marries itself to what it studies. It is achieved by letting oneself stretch between the real-world conference room and the virtual world of a model (diagram, computer simulation, even a theory). This stretched being, this in-between being, is a nodal point of the deepest form of understanding. From this understanding stems a good deal of the rest of the physicist's theoretical understandings and practical skills.

This form of understanding—this embodied empathy for a complex system—has heretofore been reserved only for the highest reaches of professional standing and training. But such embodied empathy for a complex system is precisely what video game technology allows players to achieve. It is one of many examples of where video games allow young people to engage in what have heretofore been seen as professional practices and professionals ways of thinking and understanding (there are many others).

We have, of course, barely begun to explore the potential of video games to allow learners to achieve this form of depthful understanding in domains like the natural, physical, and social sciences where so many learners are left out of deep understandings. Of course, all good commercial games achieve this level of understanding all the time, even if educators may not value as fully as I do the complex problem-space of a game like *Onimusha 3: Demon Siege*. At the same time, there are examples in commercial games of embodied empathy for complex systems that can achieve goals we do associate more closely with education, at least as we currently conceive it.

I am hesitant, though, to give an example, because I fear the game's designers will take any tie whatsoever to education, given the reputation of edutainment, as a commercial curse. The easy example is *Pokemon* (perhaps the best literacy curriculum ever conceived). But let me take *Deus Ex: Invisible War* instead. In *Invisible War* you find (and/or buy) biomod canisters throughout the game that can be implanted into your characters (J. C. Denton's clone, Alex D) to give the character certain special abilities, such as becoming invisible to bots, being able to hack into computer systems, immunity to poison, greater speed or strength, and many more. Using one implant means having to forego other possible implants, representing different abilities, at that implant spot, though players can later dump implants they have chosen and reconfigure themselves with other ability canisters.

One cannot play *Invisible War* in any thoughtful way without becoming aware that the abilities one finds or buys and chooses to implement greatly affect how one plays the game and how the game world plays out for your character. The game world, in the sense of how the world looks, feels, and reacts to your character (and, thus, to you as stretched into the game) differs greatly depending on how you have implemented your abilities or reconfigured them.

Players become even more aware of this fact when they watch other players who have configured their abilities differently play *Invisible War*. It becomes clear, for instance, that advice you give them, based on how you played the game, won't work because the world they are interacting with is a different world than the one with which you interacted, since they have implement different abilities.

Invisible War allows the player to gain empathetic understanding of the ways in which our own abilities and the seemingly "outside" world are married. They are married in the sense that how we see the world and how the world acts back on us are, in part, products of our actions and abilities. This insight, by the way, has been widely applied to the relationship between animals and their ecological niches, allowing us to see an interactive relationship here rather than static individual entities.

Now this embodied understanding of how our experience of the world is married to the structure of our abilities and partly a product of this structure is already a deep insight about a particularly important complex system. But it is also a major theme of *Invisible War*. *Invisible War*, at the story level, asks the gamer to think about a world (much like ours) in which the rich buy abilities for their children (say by buying them better education than other children can get) that shape their worlds to bring them greater power and status than other people. The gamer is asked, also, to think about how this situation could be resolved—for example, would one want a world in which we used biological enhancements to make every person have equal abilities so that differential abilities would play no role in making some people more successful or better off than others?

Of course, *Invisible War* makes the player think about this inside the trajectory of action and decision taken in the game world, so, it becomes a question asked and answered by the third being stretched between the real person (the gamer) and the virtual character (Alex D). It becomes a question asked and answered by the real-virtual being the game play produces, a being now used as a tool for thought and reflection, though, of course, the answer has to be given within the logic of our embodied participation in the game.

So *Invisible Wars* marries its thematic/story world to the very sort of embodied empathy for a complex system that it creates as game play. This issue of ability and hierarchy in society is one that I, like many others in education and the social sciences, have dealt with. *Invisible Wars* is a high-level academic contribution to this issue, as far as I am concerned, certainly better than many academic journal contributions, though that is not the only or main reason I like it as a gamer. It is, in that sense, alas, an educational game—but we should keep the matter to ourselves. I would hate to see publishers stop publishing such games, just because they are doing the best that the best video games can do to enhance people's minds by where the game allows players to put their real-virtual bodies.

Let me offer one important proviso. Games and science are, at their best, social activities, supported by communities of practice. The play (work) of gamers and the work (play) of scientists exist inside wider activity systems in which people use a variety of tools and interact in a variety of ways with fellow gamers and scientists (Hutchins 1995). We need always to look at the game or the work as part of bigger packages. If we want to know whether the game or the work is good for learning and understanding—and for what learning and understanding—we need to ask these questions about the whole package, not the game or a piece of work as isolated from other tools and interactions. I have already pointed out that watching another person play *Invisible War* after you have played yourself is an eye-opening experience. Now the fused being, the product of your own play, stands outside and looks at the system with new eyes.

So let us return to strategy games like *Rise of Nations*. Games like *Rise of Nations* allow players to take a perspective looking down on a whole world composed of diverse civilizations. From this god-like perspective, players meld their growing skills and knowledge as world builders with the many smart characters and objects they control in the game.

The farmers, soldiers, miners, university professors, training centers, plants, and vehicles the player controls each have their own in-built skills and knowledge. They know how to do certain things (e.g., farm, fight, mine, produce trained soldiers or manufacture types of vehicles). Each character and object also has the capacity to change and develop new skills with every advancing age. Players must integrate their own growing skills with those built into the characters and objects in the game. They also have to integrate their own changes and development across each new age with the changes these characters and objects are making. You don't use the same strategies when you have nuclear weapons than when you have along soldiers with slings and rocks.

Because the player shares both professional skills and knowledge (world building) and a developmental capacity (the ability to change and gain new skills and use new strategies over time) with the characters and objects in the game, players of strategy games are gaining embodied empathy with a complex system in a very special and important way. First of all, in such games we have a system in which players have to worry about the relationships among any and all characters and objects in his or her own civilization. Players have to worry about how different types of troops fit with each other to make the best army. They have to worry about how various skills and technologies they have at their service, rooted in their characters, buildings, and industries, fit together to make the best resource base for their civilization. They have to worry about how their various towns and cities, spread out across the map, fit together to make an well integrated civilization, capable of defending itself and developing.

In games like *Rise of Nations*, players have to worry, as well, about how different types of troops will allow for good strategies not just as they are here and how, but as they will develop across time, all the while always engaged in relationships with the other sorts of troops available. Players have to worry about how various skills and technologies rooted in their character, buildings, and industries will serve as a good foundation for future development. They have to worry about their various towns and cities are best placed for now and for the future.

In other words, in such games players must think spatially (how are things integrated and related on the whole map here and now) and temporally (how should things develop over time and how should these developments be put to best use). Players must think about a myriad of complex relationships in two dimensions, spatially in the here and now, as a static system, and temporally over developmental time, as a dynamic system. Furthermore, they must always integrate these two perspectives.

This is heady stuff indeed. This type of thinking is the very hallmark and foundation of the deepest and most complicated thinking in the sciences. Biologists, physicists, and social scientists must think in these sorts of ways in order to study the complex systems they engage with. They, too, use smart tools (and often simulations) to do this—remembering that every character and object in *Rise of Nations* is a smart tool, built with skills for the here and now and for future development.

So, players of strategy games like *Rise of Nations* are gaining insight into complex systems. But they are doing this in a very special way. The sort of embodiment that games *Rise of Nations* achieve is different and special. In games like *Onimusha 3: Demon Siege* the player feels connected to a single character—Samanosuke Akechi—embedded as the central actor in the game world and, thus, has empathy for the complex system that the game constitutes from deep inside the guts of the game. However, in games like *Rise of Nations* the player is both integrated with each character and object in the game (of which there a great many, indeed), since the player shares both professional skills and a developmental capacity with each of these, but is also placed up above and looking down on the whole world, like a god.

This creates a simultaneous inside/outside viewpoint or perspective. While such a perspective is present in all video games of the sort we have discussed, it is particularly salient in games like *Rise of Nations*. This inside/outside perspective—this both up close and personal and up above and looking down on the whole thing perspective—is often supported by the ability to use the mouse wheel to focus in on a single character or small set or to focus up and out to see larger sets of things. This inside/outside perspective seems particular akin to the sort of perspective scientists studying complex systems need to take. Like the physicists we looked at earlier, such scientists think about complex systems both as if they were able to see from the perspective of actors and actions within them and as if they were looking at the whole system all at once. After all, they are trying to create theories that capture both perspectives, namely, how and why individual events happen and how the system as a whole functions to help see such individual events as emergent properties of the system.

It is obvious, I would think, that there is nothing about the ways in which a game like *Rise of Nations* recruits thinking and learning that could not be done in school. In this case, games and game-like things themselves are likely to be quite useful, since scientists studying complex systems themselves often use and think through simulations. However that may be, students, if they are understand science, for example, deeply, must learn to think spatially and temporally, to take a simultaneous inside/outside perspective, indeed, to see complex systems in the real world as akin to real-time strategy spaces.

Morrowind

CHAPTER EIGHT

THE ELDER SCROLLS III: MORROWIND

Role-Playing, Identity, and *The Elder Scrolls III: Morrowind*

In Chapter 4 we argued that authentic professionalism, shared out between a player and a game's character(s), opens up a space to take strategy and identity to new heights. In Chapter 6, we saw how a game like *Rise of Nations* extends the strategy element of games like *Full Spectrum Warrior*, *Thief*, and *Riddick*. *Rise of Nations* accomplishes this by adding two additional features to the shared authentic professionalism found in such games.

First, it rises up above the perspective of one character or even a small number of them to a god-like perspective looking down on a whole world. The player controls a plethora of characters and objects. This makes the virtual characters and objects in the game tools for working out extended strategies across a good deal of virtual space and time. Second, it adds a shared developmental capacity between the player and the virtual characters and objects. Both the player and the virtual characters and objects in the game have the potential and necessity to develop and change; they become capable of doing new things as the game goes on.

In Chapter 6 we argued that the shared developmental capacity in a game like *Rise of Nations* allows for a fourth story—in addition to the designer's story (the first story), each player's own trajectory through the game (the second story), and the character-player's career as a authentic professional (the third story). The fourth story is the story of the history the characters/objects in the game and the player enact through developmental time. The existence of these multiple stories in games like *Rise of Nations* opens up a very wide scope for strategy, indeed—strategy at the level of trajectory, career, and history and in terms of how all three are integrated.

But there is another way to add history to a game, another way to share out a developmental capacity between the virtual character and the player. In this case, though, the history is not world history, the history of a civilization, but, rather, an individual life history. It is here that identity comes into yet fuller play in video games.

Strategy games like *Rise of Nations* allow players to manipulate a plethora of virtual characters and objects from a god-like perspective, each of which shares an ability to develop over time with the player. However, these games, just like *Full Spectrum Warrior*, *Thief*, and *Riddick*, start from an already well defined and delineated set of authentic professional skills that are shared out between the player and the virtual character(s). This professional expertise is military expertise in *Full Spectrum Warrior*, thieving-sneaking expertise in *Thief*, and hard-ass-prison-escapee expertise in *Riddick*. *Rise of Nations* starts from world building/world beating expertise.

Role playing games like *The Elder Scrolls III: Morrowind* start with characters that are close to being blank slates. Such games offer players a range of potential professional abilities and skills from which they must choose, building a profession for their character step-by-step throughout the game. At the outset of the game, the player chooses certain abilities and skills that predispose the character to develop faster and better in certain ways than others. As the character and player gain experience through actions in the game, new choices open up and the player builds his or her character further, developing certain abilities and skills (often concentrating on ones for which the character is already predisposed, thanks to the player's initial choices) and not developing in certain other areas. Such games can sometimes have more than one character, thereby allowing the player to make choices for multiple characters.

In role-playing games like *Morrowind*, the player must build an authentic professional expertise for his or character, choosing from the range of possible abilities and skills offered by the game. This professional expertise is built up over time. The character-player gradually becomes, for example, a particular type of alchemist mage of the player's own choosing. This alchemist mage may, over time, become, for instance, good at magic, but not at close-combat fighting; good at persuading others, but poor at stealth and sneaking; skilled at making potions and medicines, but prone to getting ill and suffering from poisons, and so on and so forth through a number of other attributes. The player and the virtual character share a developmental capacity, but here a capacity to develop as a certain sort of person in a certain sort of profession (called a "class" in role-playing games).

The virtual character has the capacity to develop in many different ways over time—getting stronger, smarter, and more skilled over time. The player must choose how this development works and must develop the character in a coherent way over time so that the character becomes well-skilled and knowledgeable in one particular domain or in closely related set of them. The virtual character becomes an authentic professional built from the ground up by the player, though built out of the range of possibilities designed into the character and the game by the game's designers. Mixing and matching abilities, skills, and forms of knowledge that don't really go together or trying to become an evenly balanced "jack of all trades", adequate at everything, good at nothing, won't work in these games. You've got to become *something*, not just anything or everything.

As the player-virtual character develops over time, they can do more and more in the game; they become more and more powerful and effective in the game's world. This course of development, different for each player, affects the trajectory the player-character takes through the game space (the second story) and the career the player-character enacts as an authentic professional, say a professional alchemist mage (the third story). But this course of development is also a personal life history for the player-character. So, here, too, a history is enacted (the fourth story), but this time the history of an individual or a small band of individuals, since role-playing games like *Icewind Dale: Forgotten Realms* and *Baldur's Gate II: Shadows of Amn* allow the player to develop several characters in a small group.

Since games like *The Elder Scrolls III: Morrowind* allow players to make and live out life histories, they open up a great space of making decisions about, thinking about, and playing with identity. Who do I want the player-character to be—that is, What do I want myself and the character to be? What sort of authentic professional do I want us to become? What do I want us to have accomplished and how do I want us to have accomplished it over time and by the end of our life history? What values and attitudes do I want us to have developed, expressed, and, maybe, too, later rejected? What changes and transformations do I want us to have undergone? How do I want us to handle ourselves in crises?

Note, here, that I (the player) am reflecting on what I want myself as I blend with the virtual character to be and become. In a quite delicious way (this is true in many types of video games, like *Thief* and *Riddick*, but particularly true in role-playing games) I both stay separate from the virtual character (it's me doing the reflecting here, influenced by my own real life, as well as my own fantasies and desires) and meld with the character, as well (it's us that acts and develops over time).

When *Thief* or *Riddick* starts, Garrett and Riddick are already developed, already skilled and knowledgeable in their professions. Garrett can sneak and steal right from the start. Riddick is one very tough SOB the moment he arrives at Butcher Bay. But the character I played in the *Elder Scrolls III: Morrowind* started with no name and was so weak and unskilled that she could barely beat up a snail or a fish (indeed, early on, on her first venture out of town, she got seriously injured by a fish). By the end of the game she was a match for the most powerful gods and demons in her world (though this game does not really end—you can stay in the Morrowind forever).

My character and I had a career in *The Elder Scrolls III: Morrowind*. We started with few skills and little knowledge and built up into what I would call a "battle-mage" of a very specific sort. My character—Bead was her name—was, in the end, a powerful warrior with sword, shield, and heavy armor, but adept enough at magic for emergencies. She used her skills for good, helping the weak and harming the stronger, but was never above lock picking and stealing to gain necessary funds and good weapons and armor. She was no good at fighting by hand, was not the most persuasive being I've known, couldn't mix a good potion if you paid her, was rather slow, and her magic skills didn't really impress professional mages in the game. She was also quite bad at finding places using the available maps—a deficit I must admit she inherited almost entirely from me.

Bead's history (really Bead-me's history) had many interesting episodes in it. Lots of memories for good storytelling by the fire once the game life was over. My most salient memory—though I have many strong ones—is this: At one point, when Bead was already quite powerful and wore the most beautiful and powerful armor, she had to get some information from a politically powerful man. She could not, of course, kill him, since the information would die with him. He was imperious to physical threats. She was not persuasive enough to talk him into giving up the information and she did not have any magic skills that would work on him. Dirty old man that he was, he told her that if she would take off her clothes he would give her the information.

Bead and I were quite conflicted about this. It was embarrassingly shameful for us to take off our clothes, especially since we were a powerful warrior (albeit one with a perfectly good body). Nonetheless, with deep regret, we disrobed and got the information. Then we put our clothes back on, picked up our sword and killed the man, killed him with rage and joy in our heart. For good measure, we wiped out his lackeys on the way out. This event—the conflicts we felt, the decisions we made—is one important marker in our history. It was an important stage in Bead-me becoming who we became. Note that this event could not have happened earlier in the game, because at that point Bead and I would have been too weak to have killed the politician and his henchmen.

Another important stage was the time we got caught stealing a great weapon from a museum by a guard that we (inadvertently?) killed. We felt guilty about this to the end, though reveled in the weapon for some time. Many times we wished we had re-played that part of the game to clear our record.

In a game like *The Elder Scrolls III*, a character-player combination has a life history because the player designs his or her character from a palette of choices offered by the game's designer's. But this character does not come forth fully formed. The character—in tandem with the player's abilities and desires—is a bundle of potential, capable of growth along many different lines. As the character earns experience through actions in the game world, the player continually makes choices as to how the character will develop ("level up").

All this means that events in the game are time sensitive in two different ways. First, the character is significantly different at different time periods, so the player can track the character-player's life history in this respect. Second, many actions and events in the game are contingent on the character being at a certain level of development or having a certain skill or ability developed to a certain level. This means that there can be a little historical story for each of these actions, a story of the time when I couldn't' do them (and this fact has certain consequences) and a time when I could (and this fact, in turn, has certain consequences). This becomes another thread in the player-character's life history.

For example, when I played *The Elder Scrolls III: Morrowind* I came upon a old knight in armor in a desolate valley. He was a fearsomely strong warrior, but was tired of his life of fighting. He offered me his sword and armor, which were very good items, if I would fight him fair and square and kill him. He wanted to die in battle. I badly wanted his armor and sword, but at that point clearly saw, after I tried, that we (Bead and me) had no chance whatsoever of beating him. I knew we did not, at that point in the game, have what it took in terms of skills and abilities we needed.

As we went on in the game and gradually leveled up step by step, we periodically returned to the old knight to test if we were strong enough now and if certain skills we had built up over time (e.g., archery) would now work or if they still needed to be increased or other skills all together were required. We tried many many things (all sorts of combinations of archery, magic, melee fighting, and scrolls) and failed many times. Eventually the day came, in the real world and the virtual world, where we (the character-and-me) were skilled and strong enough to beat the knight. He died with dignity as a brave warrior, as he wished, and we got his sword and armor.

So here we see that an event takes on a whole little developmental story of its own, because it is tied to the development of my character and my own growing skills as a player in the game. In the sort of action game where characters don't level up, games like *Riddick* and other first-person shooters, defeating an enemy is, of course, tied to your skills as a player and this develops over time. But you usually fight the enemy then and there over and over until you win or you can't go on with the game. Sometimes you can run from the enemy, but in that case you often will never come back to fight him.

There are action games—such as *Castlevania: Symphony of the Night*—where the character levels up and gets stronger (and so can kill types of enemies easily that used to be hard), but where the player does not make any choices about how the character starts life or how the character develops as he or she levels up (the game simply dictates these things). But games like *Riddick* and like *Castlevania* lack a sense of character-player joint development over time, the sense of building and living a personal history of growth.

How It Works

Let's take a moment and look at how a player builds a character in a game like The *Elder Scrolls III: Morrowind*. When you start the game you first pick a "race" for your character (and then choose a gender, face, and hair style). These races are, of course, not types of humans, but of a variety of different sorts of fantasy creatures. Here are four of the ten races from which you can choose:

Argonian	This amphibious reptilian race is blessed with intelligence, speed, and agility. It is predisposed toward sorcery and thievery
Breton	This race has high intelligence and willpower and is particularly suited to use magic. In addition to its skill in sorcery, it has a natural resistance to spells
Dark Elf	It is known for its strength, intelligence, and speed. This race is skilled with both magic and weapons
Wood Elf	The agility and speed of this mischievous race gives it a natural inclination toward thievery. It is also particularly skilled in archery

Each race looks different and each one has different initial advantages and disadvantages. So Argonians are more intelligent, faster, and more agile than other races and they are predisposed to be good at sorcery and stealing. While they share intelligence and speed with Dark Elves, the Dark Elves are stronger and the Argonians more agile. Both Argonians and Dark Elves are good at magic (sorcery), but the Dark Elves are better at using weapons and the Argonians at stealing. What this means is that different characters start the game with different initial ability levels for abilities or attributes like Agility, Intelligence, Endurance, Luck, Personality, Speed, Strength. And Willpower.

In turn, these abilities or attributes predispose a character to be good at certain skills, and not others, in the large areas of Combat Skills (things like being able to wear heavy armor, fix weapons, block attacks, and use long swords), Magic Skills (things like alchemy, telekinesis, summoning other creatures, using magic to harm others or to restore one's health) and Stealth Skills (things like being able to pick locks, to sneak, to use speechcraft to persuade or intimidate, or to use range weapons like arrows to attack from a distance). For instance, Agility predisposes a character to be good at the following skills: Block, Light Armor, Marksman, and Sneak. Intelligence predisposes a character to be good at these skills: Alchemy, Conjuration, Enchant, and Security.

So, at this point, after the player has chosen a race for his or her character, the character has a "nature", a set of initial abilities and predispositions to be skilled in certain areas and not others. These abilities and skills are all represented by numbers. So, if I chose to be an Argonian, here is how I would initially look in terms of abilities and skills. If I chose another race, I would like quite different:

Description:

Little is known and less is understood about the reptilian denizens of Black Marsh. Years of defending their borders have made the Argonians experts in guerilla warfare, and their natural abilities make them equally at home in water and on land. They are well-suited for the treacherous swamps of their homeland, and have developed natural immunities to the diseases and poisons that have doomed many would-be explorers into the region. Their seemingly expressionless faces belie a calm intelligence, and many Argonians are well-versed in the magical arts. Others rely on stealth or steel to survive, and their natural agility makes them adept at either. They are, in general, a reserved people, slow to trust and hard to know. Yet, they are fiercely loyal, and will fight to the death for those they have named as friends.

Base Attributes								
	Str	Int	Wil	Agi	Spd	End	Per	Lck
Female	40	50	40	40	40	30	30	40
Male	40	40	30	50	50	30	30	40

Initial Racial Skill Bonuses		Special Powers/Abilities	
Medium Armor (Combat) (Endurance)	+5	Resist Disease 75%	Inherent Ability
Spear (Combat) (Endurance)	+5	Immune to Poison 100%	Inherent Ability
Athletics (Combat) (Speed)	+15	Water Breathing (120 secs)	Spell
Illusion (Magic) (Personality)	+5		
Mysticism (Magic) (Willpower)	+5		
Alchemy (Magic) (Intelligence)	+5		
Unarmored (Magic) (Speed)	+5		

After choosing a race, the player makes up a class (profession) for the character, or chooses a class from a list of pre-given classes. Classes are defined around the sort of "occupation" or "profession" the character will take up and develop in. Regardless of race, any character could become, for example, a Knight specializing in combat, a Mage specializing in magic, or a Battlemage specializing in magic, but with some predisposition to melee fighting with weapons, as well, or yet other things. Of course, some races are somewhat better suited for certain occupations than are others.

Each different class specializes in some skills within one of three large skill areas: Combat, Magic, and Stealth, each of which contains many specific skills. The choice of class gives the character a boost in skills in the chosen area, determining which skills the character will develop in most rapidly (since these skills start at a higher level). Additionally, as part of building a class for the character, the player gets to choose two abilities or attributes to favor further beyond the benefits already given by race (out of Agility, Intelligence, Endurance, Luck, Personality, Speed, Strength. And Willpower). These become the character's strongest abilities and, in turn, further shape the character's skills. Finally, the player also gets to pick five skills to which to give a major boost (major skills) and five skills to which to give a minor boost (minor skills).

As we have said, these choices create a "class" or profession for the character, a profession in which they character must, of course, develop over time. So the matter of the character's initial class is more a matter of predisposition for certain sorts of future growth than a present reality. Of course, the player tries to make choices (initially and throughout the game) that are coherent and fit well together in order to make a character that can be pretty specialized in a few areas and not a simple "jack of all trades". There are pre-given classes that players can choose from, if they don't want to make the choices themselves.

Below I show six classes or professions of the many possibilities. The names are somewhat arbitrary; they simply try to capture the nature of the character's profession by a single label:

```
KNIGHT
-------------------------------------------------------------------
SPECIALIZATION           | MAJOR SKILLS      | MINOR SKILLS
 Combat                  | Long Blade        | Restoration
-------------------------| Axe               | Mercantile
FAVORITE ATTRIBUTES      | Speechcraft       | Medium Armor
 Strength                | Heavy Armor       | Enchant
 Personality             | Block             | Armorer
-------------------------------------------------------------------


ROGUE
-------------------------------------------------------------------
SPECIALIZATION           | MAJOR SKILLS      | MINOR SKILLS
 Combat                  | Short Blade       | Block
-------------------------| Mercantile        | Medium Armor
FAVORITE ATTRIBUTES      | Axe               | Speechcraft
 Speed                   | Light Armor       | Athletics
 Personality             | Hand-to-hand      | Long Blade
-------------------------------------------------------------------


AGENT
-------------------------------------------------------------------
SPECIALIZATION           | MAJOR SKILLS      | MINOR SKILLS
 Stealth                 | Speechcraft       | Mercantile
-------------------------| Sneak             | Conjuration
FAVORITE ATTRIBUTES      | Acrobatics        | Block
 Personality             | Light Armor       | Unarmored
 Agility                 | Short Blade       | Illusion
-------------------------------------------------------------------


ASSASSIN
-------------------------------------------------------------------
SPECIALIZATION           | MAJOR SKILLS      | MINOR SKILLS
 Stealth                 | Sneak             | Security
-------------------------| Marksman          | Long Blade
FAVORITE ATTRIBUTES      | Light Armor       | Alchemy
 Speed                   | Short Blade       | Block
 Intelligence            | Acrobatics        | Athletics
-------------------------------------------------------------------


BATTLEMAGE
-------------------------------------------------------------------
SPECIALIZATION           | MAJOR SKILLS      | MINOR SKILLS
 Magic                   | Alteration        | Mysticism
-------------------------| Destruction       | Long Blade
FAVORITE ATTRIBUTES      | Conjuration       | Marksman
 Intelligence            | Axe               | Enchant
 Strength                | Heavy Armor       | Alchemy
-------------------------------------------------------------------


HEALER
-------------------------------------------------------------------
SPECIALIZATION           | MAJOR SKILLS      | MINOR SKILLS
 Magic                   | Restoration       | Illusion
-------------------------| Mysticism         | Alchemy
FAVORITE ATTRIBUTES      | Alteration        | Unarmored
 Willpower               | Hand-to-hand      | Light Armor
 Personality             | Speechcraft       | Blunt Weapon
-------------------------------------------------------------------
```

After picking a race and class for the character, the player then picks a Sign under which the character was born, where each sign gives certain advantages or disadvantages. For example, the sign of The Lover gives 25 points to Agility and gives the character the power to use Lover's Kiss, a magic that paralyzes the target, but fatigues the character. There are many different Signs from which to choose.

What comes out of all this in the end is a set of initial numbers (ability and skill levels, plus some initial powers and weaknesses). This is the starting point for the character's development. All characters start as pretty weak creatures. However, obviously, in those areas (abilities and skills) where a character starts with higher numbers, the character will develop to yet higher levels faster than in areas where the starting numbers are lower. As characters act in the world, every once in a while their experience gains them the ability to "level up". At these points, the player gets to choose which abilities and skills to increase (usually favoring ones that are already fairly well developed, but not always).

In *Morrowind*, players can choose later in the game to develop abilities and skills that started low and they can also buy training from NPCs (non-playing characters manipulated by the computer) in specific skills and develop in new areas. A player could even choose eventually to change the class of his or her character pretty significantly as time went on, though this will mean playing longer in order to develop enough in the new skills the player now wants to have.

What all this means is that there is a massive array of possible characters with which the player can start the game. These characters, as they level up and train—each at different times and different places in the game world—become yet more and more different from other possible characters, even ones that may have started the game as fairly similar or identical. Not long into the game, no two characters are alike. Since the characters' abilities and skills, advantages and disadvantages, determine what they can and cannot do in the game and how they do what they do, no two games are the same for any two players.

The game will differ greatly for different players, as well, because of all the choices the game offers players as part of game play. The player's character can join one or more different guilds and factions in the game, each of which has different sorts of alliances with and animosities towards the other guilds and factions. Each guild and faction offers the player-character different quests to carry out, that is different jobs the player-character can do. In turn, these quests allow the player-character to earn experience and level up.

Each guild or faction favors certain sorts of abilities and skills, as well as certain beliefs and values the character must display. If the player-character is weak in magic, joining the Mages' Guild is out of question. It won't do to join the Imperial Legion if you oppose the government and joining the Thieves' Guild does not make you popular with members of the other guilds and factions from whom you steal (you are advised not to steal from members of guilds and factions to which you belong, including the Thieves' Guild—they will throw you out). You can free slaves and eventually join the Twin Lamps anti-slavery society or you can join a Great House (become a retainer for an extended rich family), some of which engage in slavery.

In my game, I joined the Fighters' Guild, of which I eventually became the leader, working my way up from the bottom. The Thieves' Guild wouldn't take me, since work I had done for the Imperial Legion has angered them. The Mages wouldn't take me, since what magic I had, while perfectly suitable for my purposes in the Fighters Guild, was not up to their standards.

In *The Elder Scrolls III: Morrowind* there are "main quests" (some given to you by Caius Cosades, a member of The Blades, a secretive organization you find out about early on in the game). These main quests advance the game's story (the designer's story) and doing all of them will finish that story. Here is just a very small part of that story:

> The Emperor sends you (a just freed prisoner) to Morrowind to fulfill an ancient prophecy and become the reincarnation of a long-dead hero. The prophecies are incomplete and obscure, so to succeed, you must first find the missing clues. The prophecies also say to beware of a mysterious Morrowind cult called the Sixth House that worships Dagoth Ur, the immortal nemesis of Dunmer religion and an ancient enemy of Nerevar. You are therefore ordered to prepare yourself to face the threat of the Sixth House and Dagoth Ur.

> The Emperor places you under the orders of the head of Imperial Intelligence in Vvardenfell, Caius Cosades, the Spymaster. Following the Emperor's orders, the Spymaster sends you to investigate the background and activities of the Cult of the Nerevarine and the Sixth House.

> You learn that the Cult of the Nerevarine awaits a prophesied hero called the Incarnate, a reincarnation of the ancient Dunmer Hero Nerevar—and evidence confirms the Emperor's belief that you may be the object of the prophecies. Also, the Sixth House and Dagoth Ur are the source of a supernatural blight that threatens to overwhelm the land of Morrowind and every living thing upon it.

However, there are a huge number of other quests and things to do in the massive world of Morrowind (made all the more massive by expansions to *Morrowind*, namely *The Elder Scrolls III: Bloodmoon* and *The Elder Scrolls III: Tribunal*). Players need not ever do the main quests, can do them any time they want (and are powerful enough to accomplish them), and can stay in the world even when the designer's story is over.

So a game like *The Elder Scrolls III* has a first story, a designer's story. This story can be more or less important to a given player. Some players will attempt to move through the story quickly, others slowly, others never. Much of what you do in the game has no direct connection to the designer's story, though that story, of course, helps create a feeling, imagery, and meaning for the world you are in and what happens in it.

The Elder Scrolls III has a second story with a vengeance, a wildly different trajectory for each character-player. There are things and places in my game that you, with a very different character and having made different choices than me, will never see. Equally, there are things and places in your game I will never see. Even what we have both done will have been done in different ways at quite different times. My movement through the game and yours are very different indeed. The story I will tell about where I have been, when, and why, and what I did there is going to be quite different than yours.

The Elder Scrolls III has a third story, a professional career for myself and my character, enacted together, using knowledge and skills that are distributed between us. But, in this case, I have formed and built the profession of my character from the ground up. I made decisions about what abilities and skills my character would have at the beginning. I have chosen a "class" for them, which is really a profession (e.g., Battlemage). In turn, I develop this profession throughout the game. I can change it in various ways either in terms of relatively small tweaks or larger transformations. I must solve problems in the game using tactics and strategies that flow from my chosen class or profession. If you have chosen a different class, and built it up throughout the game differently than me, then you will use different tactics and strategies, sometimes on the same problems I have dealt with, sometimes on different problems altogether.

In *Morrowind*, my character knows some things and has some skills I don't need to know, but which I need to know how to put to proper use. In turn, I know some things the character doesn't and have certain skills that the characters needs to carry out. We have distributed knowledge. For example, my character might know how to mix ingredients to make potions (alchemy), but I need to know when to make these potions and how to put them to good use. This is, as I have said before, what gives rise to our (the character and mine) shared authentic professionalism and to our having a joint professional career.

So you and I, at the end of the day, will have different stories to tell about how our own professional knowledge and skills were put into play, across time, to solve problems and succeed. We will each have a story to tell about how this professional knowledge originated and developed over time through our own choices and opportunities in the game.

The Elder Scrolls III also has a fourth story, as well, a history. How I and my character developed and changed over time and how this affected what we could and did do at various times and places becomes our own unique life history. I remember when even a fish could threaten me, I remember that battle I barely won in Gnsis and the one I later won handily in Balmora. I remember clearly that time I couldn't cross the bridge, because I was too weak to defeat the guy holding it.

I remember that time I could have made out like a bandit if only I had better locking-picking skills. I remember the time I was just not good enough at Speechcraft to get a slave owner to free his slaves, so I had to kill him. I remember the feeling of triumph as I sailed through that quest in Tel Mora. I remember the time I felt shame having to disrobe, but joy at being strong enough to kill the man who made me do it. I remember when I decided I just had to develop more skills in sneaking, though it was not something I was really predisposed to be good at. In the end, I remember having lived a life, having eventually become a good Battlemage, through circuitous routes, and having done much else that constituted an eventful history as a certain sort of person.

The first main quest in *Morrowind*, which you get when you eventually find Caius Cosades, involves getting over a bridge (in order to carry out the quest on the other side) held by a man who can summon a skeleton to fight with him. After many conversations with NPCs in the game and my long travels to the city where Caius Cosades was to be found, I wanted to "make progress" in the game. So I rushed off to do this quest. What I quickly discovered is that there was no way in heaven I could beat that man and get across that bridge.

What the game was saying to me at this point was "You need to go find a life, find things to do, have some experiences, level up and develop, begin to become something coherent, and then you can come back and get this guy and his pet skeleton". Many players become disoriented in *Morrowind* at this point. It's a big world, with lots to do and become, and at this point there is no one to tell you what to do, what's right and what's wrong, where to go and not go. This is open-endedness with a vengeance. It's a big world and you are a little person—albeit one with a bright future, if you can stay alive, grow, and become good at some coherent profession. You, the player, are now responsible for making up your own game.

So I wandered around, talking to people, going places, joining guilds, doing tasks, making choices about who and what I wanted to become. The character-player that eventually returned to that bridge was a different person, more formed, but still very much a work in progress. But we were ready. The man and his skeleton were no great match for us now. Someone new had arrived in Morrowind. Someone who was ready now to make history happen. I and my character stood proudly on the bridge and then moved on.

The Elder Scrolls III: Morrowind and other role-playing games allow players to build a life history—and to create, enact, and transform an identity in the act. They allow the character and player to share and distribute not just knowledge and skills with the each other, they allow the character and player to share and distribute, as well, the capacity to develop through time via the nature of the character and the choices of the player. So, while *Rise of Nations* allows the creation of world history, by offering the player the role of god as a world builder and world beater, *The Elder Scrolls III: Morrowind* allows the creation of a personal life history by offering the player a blank slate with which to enact a life and a profession.

Pleasure in *The Elder Scrolls III: Morrowind*

What is the pleasure in this? Each human being wants to have built, over his or her lifetime, a coherent history. Each of us would like to die looking back on a coherent life story that makes sense. Furthermore, human beings want, as well, a sense that they were the hero (or, at least, a hero) in their own story. They would like to know that their story made a difference, that it mattered that they had been born, lived, and died. But to be able to make such a story of one's life, people must have and feel control over their own lives, not at all points, but certainly at many salient points in their lives.

We don't always have this sense that life makes sense. We don't always have the sense that we are the heroes of our own story. We sometimes feel, rather, like the victims of forces beyond our control, powerful forces at the level of institutions, states, cultures, and history. Sometimes, life seems a matter of fate or caprice. For some people, of course, this feeling is more pervasive than for others, often because of the very real problems of sickness, oppression, or poverty in their lives. Even those of us lucky enough to live lives of more privilege are prey to the caprice of life, to the eternal dilemmas of suffering and evil. We often feel what Camus called the "benign indifference of the universe", though it sometimes feels like active hostility.

The Elder Scrolls III: Morrowind allows each player to enter a virtual world in which there will be a senseful story to tell about one's life. You start with little power and, indeed, as a victim of the larger forces around you. You end up mastering your fate and controlling those larger forces. You actually feel and experience a sense of coherent development—things get better and better. In the end, you have a story to tell, in which you are the hero, about the differences your life made to the world.

But there is also another pleasure. In role-playing games, as in many other sorts of video games, people get to be things and live lives they could never live in reality. If experience and travel broadens, video games allow each player to have experiences and travel to places that even the rich cannot buy and keep for themselves in real life. Given that I have only one life, I will, in the real world, never know what it feels like to be a powerful woman (dark skinned, by the way) who is confronted with, and overcomes, raw male sexual and political power. *The Elder Scrolls III: Morrowind* allowed me, a real person, to add to my now multiple life histories, an event I remember well where I experienced just such a thing.

The great literary critic Kenneth Burke once called good literature "equipment for living". A good video game—most particularly a good role-playing game like *The Elder Scrolls III: Morrowind*—is equipment for playing with living. Children use play to prepare themselves for real life. All of us can do that with video games.

CHAPTER NINE

THE ELDER SCROLLS III: MORROWIND AND LEARNING

Role-playing games like *The Elder Scrolls III: Morrowind* allow players to think about and reflect on identity. Players don't do this, of course, just by sitting back in their arm chairs and thinking philosophically. Rather, they see identity as something they build through choices and actions in the game, choices and actions that affect the game world. In turn, these changes in the game world—the results of the players' choices and actions—redound back on the identity the players are building for their characters as the game goes on.

However, before discussing such role-playing games more directly, I want to turn for a moment to the whole notion of identity in our modern, high-tech, global world. Who are you? Who am I? Well both of us are different kinds of people in different contexts. We each have and switch between different identities. In that sense, we are all actors playing multiple roles in the theater of public life. I don't act and talk the same way when I am being a professor as when I am being a bird watcher as when I am being a gamer as when I am downing drinks with friends at the bar. If I did, people would think me odd, indeed.

This is not to say that there is nothing about me or you that transcends our multiple identities as husband, wife, gamer, student, doctor, bird watcher, biker, or what have you. And, of course, some of these identities are closer to our hearts than are others. But our "core identity"—the thing that gives some unity to all our other identities through life—itself changes as we learn new identities or drop old ones.

People used to live in a world where their identities were strictly fixed. In the Middle Age, peasants, knights, and kings usually inherited their roles and had to play them pretty much "by the book", in many cases that book was the Bible; in a larger sense it was their own cultural assumptions (Kantor 2004). When I was born in San Jose, California in 1948 there was certainly much more flexibility and mobility than the Middle Ages, but, nonetheless, what one was and was to become was still pretty much a "by the book" affair.

I was raised a devote Catholic and we knew pretty clearly what it meant to be a Catholic. People who didn't like Catholics, of which there were many, but none of whom I ever saw since I only saw Catholics, themselves had strong views about what it meant to be a Catholic. People had pretty fixed ideas about what it meant to be a family, to be a husband or a wife, a male or a female, to be middle class or working class, to be an American, to be an

Italian-American or an African-American (they were supposed to stay in the background, to be seen but not heard). One could change identities much more readily than in the Middle Ages, of course, but it wasn't easy and the identities were still pretty fixed, the scripts still pretty tight.

One's identity—being a father, a mother, a Catholic, a doctor, a professor, a worker, an Italian-American or an African-American—determined how one was expected to talk and act. These things were supposed to be predicable. Of course, things were never as fixed in reality as they were in people's stereotypes and expectations, but television shows like *Leave to Beaver* captured one of the paradigms by which people judged themselves, other people, and the world around them.

To be sure there were people who didn't fit well with the prevailing paradigms—gay men, divorced fathers, single mothers, non-subservient African-Americans, socialist priests—but, then, that's the whole point of paradigms: they define who is "normal" and who isn't. It was much clearer in my youth who and what was "normal" than it is now. The view of "normal" was clearer and far more narrow.

Things are different today. People are expected, more than ever, to fashion themselves (Bauman 2000; Beck 1992; Giddens 1991; Taylor 1992, 1994). They are supposed to make up for themselves (using the social, institutional, and cultural resources at their disposal, of course) what it means to be a male or female, a priest or doctor, an Italian-American or African-American, a husband or wife, a Catholic, Protestant, Jew, or Muslim.

In fact, in the modern world, identities become consumer niches (Rifkin 2000). The modern economy doesn't want just any old "Latinos" or "Asians" or "middle-class people". No, the economy wants different types of Latinos, Asians, and middle-class people who constitute different niches for the consumption of different products and services and to whom politicians can campaign in specific ways.

There are well off people who buy neo-bugs from Volkswagen, others who buy Mercedes, and yet others who get Hummers. These are different types of people, displaying, reinforcing, and creating their identities through their car purchases and through many other objects and services they buy, as well. Males of different types shop at different stores, wear different clothes, drink different beer, marry different women (or men!), live in different types of houses and different neighborhoods. All of these are "life style" choices, markers of identity, markers of who one is or takes himself to be. The same goes for women.

It is not enough today to be a student. One has to be a distinctive type of student with distinctive experiences and achievements (e.g., having helped build houses for poor people, albeit on a Caribbean island) in order to get into a "good" college. The college one attends is no longer one's "education", it is a badge of one's merit and identity. He's a Harvard man, she's a Yale woman, and poor John, he's a Worcester State guy.

Of course, there are many down-sides to all this. But we shouldn't forget there are up-sides, as well. Earlier only the rich and elite went to Harvard. Now others in the society can vie for this niche and use it to produce themselves as new elites. The rich still have a huge advantage in going to places like Harvard, Stanford, and Yale, but these colleges are no longer as exclusively reserved for the old aristocracy as they once were.

So identities today take work. A person is expected to help create them, out of social and cultural resources, of course. A person is expected to take on new identities through life, dropping some, changing others, and taking on new ones. This is partly because of the changing nature of work and skills today (Gee, Hull, & Lankshear 1996; Greider 1997; Reich 1992). In today's world, thanks to the fast pace of change due, in part, to the workings of science and technology, any knowledge and skills one has may soon go out of date. New knowledge and skills arise at an ever faster pace. New types of jobs open up and old ones disappear (or go overseas). People can't expect to stay in the same job—moving ever gradually up the ladder—their whole lives any more.

Who, for example, would have thought, in my youth, that a major job in the world would be as a video game designer or programmer? When game design opened up, some young people were able to rearrange their skills, experiences, and views of themselves for this new niche, others could not. Some young people resisted the old categories in school enough to prepare themselves for this new work or were accidentally and luckily ready thanks to their hobbies and play.

But, then, again, on the other hand, who could know that game design and programming would become so quickly a massive industry in which formerly creative programmers came to feel like cogs in a machine as they programmed their umpteenth tree? Some are already redefining themselves and seeking more creative and rewarding work in new niches.

No, today, people must see themselves differently. Each person must see him or herself as a portfolio of skills, experiences, and achievements, something like a walking resume. People must be prepared to rearrange their skills, experiences, and achievements—to describe themselves in new ways, not in terms of one fixed role or identity—to display themselves as fit and ready for new jobs, identities, and roles as these emerge in their futures. Indeed, it has been said that what workplaces today owe their workers are not permanent jobs, but the opportunity to learn something new on the job, something to add to their portfolios for future identity changes in new workplaces in their futures. People must be prepared to recreate themselves and prepare for multiple jobs—indeed multiple careers—across their lifetimes.

Even if one keeps the same title—as I have, being a "professor—this comes to mean quite different things even in the course of one career. I could never have fathomed when I started my career at Stanford as a theoretical linguist studying the grammar of infinitives that today, many years later, I would be a professor of education in the Midwest writing on video games. Video games didn't exist when I got my PhD, let alone in my youth. In between I have morphed out of and into a number of other academic identities. In the age before I became an academic, this sort of flexibility would have been disastrous. Today, it is inevitable for those who don't want to die an early death as "dead wood". In a great many domains today those ready for such changes, those able to change and rearrange their skills, survive, the others reside in the backwater, at best.

Starting in school, young people now need to view themselves as what we might call "shape shifters". They have to be prepared throughout their lives to acquire new knowledge, skills, experiences, and achievements and to be able and willing to redefine these to make themselves ready for new jobs, new roles, and even new careers. People must be willing and able to fashion and refashion who they are. This is not necessary just for work, but in almost all aspects of life today. What it means to be married and how men and women relate to each other, for instance, change more quickly than the span of one lifetime now (Giddens 1992). So does the meaning of being religious, being a citizen, being a consumer, being an environmentalist, and so and so forth.

There is, of course, a great backlash to all this today. We see this backlash across the world in the rise of fundamentalism of all types, Christian, Islamic, Jewish, Hindu, and others. People perplexed by the complexity of the modern world and demands to think for themselves—and in some cases oppressed by the self-fashioning options other, richer, people have adopted—react by seeking certain immutable truths, truths they would like to impose on others and on the world as a whole. Indeed, this sort of backlash is only liable to grow worse as the modern world continues to create complexity and a lack of justice for the poor.

And, indeed, it is probably the case that some readers having been saying for a while now: You're only talking about rich kids and rich adults. Poor people don't get these shape-shifting luxuries and opportunities. Well, yes and no. First, consider no. Many of today's young people who are not well-off or Anglo display a keen sense of the importance of how the modern world works. Let me give but one example. Consider a young man named "Almon", a young man written about by Eva Lam (2000).

Almon emigrated to the U.S. at the age of 12 from Hong Kong. After five years in the U.S., Almon was frustrated by his skills in English. School only offered him ESL, bilingual, or remedial courses, courses which stigmatized him as a "low-achieving student". Almon felt that it was going to hard for him to develop his "career" (his own word) in the United States because of his English skills.

Eventually, Almon got involved with the Internet, created his own personal home page on a Japanese pop singer, and compiled a long list of names of on-line chat partners in several different countries around the world. He started to write regularly to a e-mail "pen pals". Almon's Internet writing eventually improved his writing in school significantly.

After his experiences with and on the Net, here is how Almon talked about himself and his future:

> ...I'm not as fearful, or afraid of the future, that I won't have a future. ... I didn't feel I belonged to this world. ... But now I feel there's nothing to be afraid of. It really depends on how you go about it. It's not like the world always has power over you. It was [names of a few chat mates and e-mail pen pals] who helped me to change and encouraged me. If I hadn't known them, perhaps I wouldn't have changed so much. ... Yeah, maybe the Internet has changed me. (p. 468)

Almon had chosen to settle his home page in the "Tokyo" section of *GeoCities* (an international server) where a global community of Asians gathers around Japanese pop culture. Almon's online chat mates were located in a wide variety of places, such as Canada, Hong Kong, Japan, Malaysia, and the United States. They were mostly girls, since he felt the girls' type of dialogue forced him to learn more English, partly because they talked about more topics and in a more personal and reflective mode.

Almon' story is one typical variety of what we have been talking about, despite the fact that he is not rich, Anglo, or "mainstream". He thinks in terms of his career and future and evaluates his current skills and experiences in that light. He gains his most important skills, experiences, and identities, including even school-based skills, outside of school (indeed, school stigmatizes and deskills him).

Eva Lam argues that the genre of electronic dialogue, as a form of communication that relies heavily on writing, "constitutes a highly visible medium for the scripting of social roles" (p. 474), that is for identity fashioning. She points out that many of Almon's postings to his female interlocutors "sound both very personal and very much like role play".

Almon not only gains new skills and develops new identities on the Net, he also learns to shape-shift, to enact different social roles.

There is no doubt that Almon, regardless of his economically-based social class, is building a portfolio and learning to think of himself in entrepreneurial terms (as witnessed by the creation of his own Web site and in his sense of free agency and control over his own destiny) and in shape-shifting terms. Connected to a young Asian Diaspora, Almon is not at the margins (expect in the eyes of the school), but at the center of the new global world.

But now for the "yes"—yes, what I have been saying can often apply more to the rich than the poor. But that is the very nature of the world I am talking about. Being able to shape shift brings big rewards, not being able to shape shift brings big costs. The rich get richer selling their ever new or newly defined skills on ever changing markets and the poor get poorer as they are left further and further behind, watching their old jobs go overseas or disappear altogether. The middle class of *Leave it to Beaver* fame is imperiled, ever pressured to rise or fall.

The dilemma is that well off kids and kids like Almon are getting their shape-shifting identities and many of the skills for their portfolios out of school, including in playing video games and interacting with the gaming community. Poor kids—white or black or anything else—are often left to trust the schools to give them shape-shifting abilities and skills for their emerging portfolios. But, schools rarely give them these. For the poor, at least, schools continue to function as if *Leave it to Beaver* was a new show or, rather, as if low-paying service jobs could replace the former high-paying union working-class jobs as a foundation for a life and a future.

Thanks to modern technology, young people today are often exposed outside of school to processes of learning that are deeper and richer than the forms of learning to which they are exposed in schools (Gee 2003). Good video games are but one example—but an important one—of this.

Take first- and third-person shooter games as an example, games often derided by politicians and policy makers, e.g., games like *Half-Life, Metal Gear Solid, Deus Ex, System Shock 2, Max Payne,* and *Far Cry*. Here are just a few (there are many more) of the learning principles that the player is (however tacitly) exposed to in learning to play these games:

- Learning is based on situated practice, not lectures and words out of context;
- There are lowered consequences for failure and taking risks (you've saved the game and can start over);
- Learning is a form of extended engagement of self as an extension of an identity to which the player is committed;

- The learner can customize the game to suit his or her style of learning;
- Problems are ordered so that the first ones to be solved in the game lead to fruitful generalizations about how to solve more complex problems later on;
- Explicit verbal information is given "just in time", when the player can make use of it, or "on demand", when the player feels ready for it and a need for it;
- Learning is interactive (the player acts on the game and the game acts back, allowing the player continually to test hypotheses and gain immediate feedback);
- There are multiple routes to solving a problem;
- There are intrinsic rewards (within the game) keyed to any player's level of expertise;
- The game operates at the outer edge of one's "regime of competence" (always doable with the resources you have at that point, never too easy);
- Skills are picked up bottom-up by playing the game, not by being drilled out of the context of play;
- Knowledge is distributed between the player's mind, the objects and environments in the game world, and other players (who help);
- Knowledge is dispersed as player's go on-line to get help and discuss strategy;
- Players must learn to think about the game world as a complex system, not "eye candy", in which things are related in many different ways and in which the player's actions can have many consequences, including unintended ones.

I could go on and on, but the point is clear I hope: imagine young people who have been immersed in this sort of learning coming to school to learn by lots of words out of any context of application with no smart tools. A rich interactive well-designed game world is replaced by a single teacher and a meaningless textbook divorced from action and interaction.

Let's now return to role-playing game like *The Elder Scrolls III: Morrowind*. Such games virtually mimic our real-world situation in today's complex, global world. The player inherits a virtual character that is close to a blank slate. The player must manage the characters skills and experiences, filling up the character's portfolio, if you like. Throughout the game, the player must seek out new skills and experience for the character and rearrange the character's abilities and skills to fit them better for new problems and opportunities in the game.

The technology behind a game like *The Elder Scrolls III: Morrowind* holds out immense implications for building new and better learning sites.

Such games allow players to build and share authentic professional expertise with their virtual character. They allow them to live out a life history with this character, developing across a life time.

However, as we have seen, the range of professions (classes) here is usually on the order of mages, knights, battlemage, healer, assassin, and so forth. There is nothing wrong with this—and I certainly hope battlemages never disappear from video games. But imagine how fruitful it would be if players could build and live careers blended with virtual characters who represented other sorts of professions? If players lived the values, choices, decisions, actions, and interactions of professions that we valued in school and out of school? If they knew and felt what it was like to have a life history in and develop in such a profession over time? Policeman, fireman, lawyer, surgeon, urban planner, disc jockey, zoo keeper, air traffic controller, house builder, television producer, biologist, physicist, spy, politician, diplomat, global financer—the list is endless.

However, I believe that the real power of role-playing games is in the ways in which they can allow people to reflect on their own identities, fantasies, and hopes in the world. Such reflection is absolutely crucial in a world where identity work and identity transformation is crucial for success, even for survival. Let me give an example that I discussed also in my book *What Video Games Have to Teach Us About Learning and Literacy* (2003).

Consider the wonderful role-playing game *Arcanum: Of Steamworks and Magick Obscura.* This is a game that takes place in a virtual world where once upon a time magic ("magick") ruled, but where technology has now arrived and magic and machines coexist in an uneasy balance. A variety of different groups—Humans, Elves, Gnomes, Dwarves, Orcs, and Ogres, as well as Half-Elves, Half-Orcs, and Half-Ogres (each of which have one Human parent)—cohabit this world, each orientating to the conflicts between magic and technology in different ways.

Arcanum, just like *The Elder Scrolls III: Morrowind* involves selecting abilities and skills for one's character and developing these over the course of the game. Role-playing games like these involve playing with identities in a very interesting way. As we have been saying throughout this book, in video games three identities are at stake. First, there is the real-world player, who, we have seen, is actually made up of many different real-world identities. Second, there is the virtual character the real-world player plays in the game world.

But third and most importantly there is the blend between the real-world character and the virtual character, what we have called the virtual-real character. This blend arises because the real-world player and the virtual character share knowledge and skills (gaming skills and sometimes professional skills and sometimes a developmental capacity) through the game is actually played.

This blend between the real-world player and the virtual character, this virtual-real identity, can create what I have called a *projective identity*, playing on two senses of the word "project". First it means "to *project* your values and desires onto the virtual character" and second, it means, as well, "seeing the virtual character as your own *project* in the making, a creature whom you imbue with a certain trajectory through time based on your aspirations for what you want that character to be and become". Role-playing games bring out this projective identity in a particularly strong and compelling way.

In *Arcanum* I played a half-elf named "Bead Bead" (yes, twice the same name as the one I used in *Morrowind*). A game like *Arcanum* allows the player certain degrees of freedom (choices) in forming the virtual character and developing her throughout the game. In playing the game, I worried about what sort of "person" I wanted Bead Bead to be, what type of history I wanted her to have had by the time I was done. I wanted this person and history to reflect my values—though I have to think reflectively and critically about these, since I have never had to project a Half-Elf onto the world before. At the same time, this person and history I was building also reflected what I have learned from playing the game and being Bead Bead in the land of Arcanum. A good role-playing game makes me think new thoughts about what I value and don't.

Let me give an example of what I mean: At one point I had Bead Bead sell a ring a dying old man had given her. I regretted this: it was not, on reflection, the sort of thing I wanted the person I desired Bead Bead to be and become to do (and note, too, that what I wanted her to be and become is not a clone of myself—in my "real" life I don't pick pockets, though Bead Bead was adept at the skill). It was not an event I wanted her to have in her history—in her trajectory through her virtual life—at the end of the day. So, I started the game again. This projected person—the kind of person I wanted Bead Bead to be, the kind of history I wanted her to have, the kind of person and history I am trying to build in and through her—is what I mean by a projective identity.

This projective identity transcends identification with characters in novels or movies, for instance, because it is both *active* (the player actively does things) and *reflexive*, in the sense that once the player has made some choices about the virtual character, the virtual character is now developed in a way that sets certain parameters about what the player can now further do. The virtual character redounds back on the player and affects his or her further actions.

As a player, I was proud of Bead Bead, at the end of the game, in a way in which I have never been proud of a character in a novel or movie, however much I had identified with them. For a character in a novel or movie, I can identify with the pride they must or should feel, given what they have done or how far they have come. But my pride in Bead Bead is tinged with pride (or, it could have been regret had things turned out differently), at various levels, in and with myself. But this pride is not (just) selfish. In a sense, it is also selfless, since it is pride at things that have transcended—taken me outside of—my real-world self (selves), if I am playing the game reflectively.

I realize that this discussion has made playing *Arcanum* or *The Elder Scrolls III: Morrowind* sound too philosophical. In fact, the beauty of games like these is that the sorts of choices, values, and decisions I have been talking about are part and parcel of playing the game. You have to shape your character some way and how you do so will change what you can and can not do in the game. You are simultaneously creating the character and the game play. Identity work is not here an armchair activity, it is reflection in action on how what "I" am and become (me blended with the virtual character) interacts with the world, each shaping the other all along through the course of the whole game and whole lifetime of the virtual-real character.

Projective identities are fun and powerful. I believe that they are the very heart of learning. Students will learn things like science deeply only if they take on projective identities as part and parcel of the learning. Only if they *project* their values, desires, hopes, and fantasies onto the identity of being a scientist of a certain sort and doing science of a certain sort, only if they seeing being a scientist of a certain sort and doing science of a certain sort as their own *project* in the making, an identity which they imbue with a certain trajectory through time based on their own aspirations for what they want to be and become, can they learn deeply in the sense that science becomes part of themselves. This is a power good role-playing games have and schools rare do.

CHAPTER TEN
CONCLUSION

Well, we've come to the end, but not really. This book could have been much longer. There are, of more types of video games that give yet other pleasures. I haven't, for example, talked about people simulations like *The Sims* (as a series, the best selling video games) or designer story-rich games like *Xenosaga: Episode I* , *Deus Ex: Invisible Wars*, or *Final Fantasy X*.

I have short-changed the designer's story in this book. In some games it plays a much bigger role than I have allowed for in the previous discussion. Like the U.S. Army "doctrine" in *Full Spectrum Warrior*, a good video game story can set the parameters for the player's fantasy work, for how players form the stories I have called their virtual-real stories (their own unique trajectory through the game), their career stories, and their histories. As in the case of "doctrine", constraint can here lead to freedom by clarifying and enhancing the meaning and nature of choice. Though, of course, player action and decision is still paramount in games with strong designer stories.

The role of story in game deserves its own book, though without much thought and reflection, based on playing games, the danger is that too early a discussion of story in game studies will fall back on what we know about the role of story in books and films. I would want to note, however, that it is not a bad thing that the role of top-down intricately pre-designed narratives is weakened in video games. Stories are not always liberating. Stories can very often encode and transmit, in a palatable form, the taken-for-granted norms and values of a social group or culture, norms and values that may well need a good deal of airing out and critique for which the traditional story form is not always the only and best vehicle.

Moving on, let me point out that not all games that bear the same label— e.g., "role-playing game"—as one of the games I have discussed in depth here is labeled are, in fact, the same. *Tales of Symphonia*, for example, bears little similarity to *The Elder Scrolls III: Morrowind*, despite the fact that it is called a role-playing game. *Tales of Symphonia* involves a team, like *Full Spectrum Warrior*, a team to which the player gives strategic advice. However, this team has some role-playing elements, which are lacking in *Full Spectrum Warrior*, though many less than in a full-blown team role-playing game like *Icewind Dale*. Finally, in *Tales*, much of the focus is on action-gaming skills as in *Castlevania*, not professional ones as in *Full Spectrum Warrior*. The creation of professional like "classes" is much weaker than in *The Elder Scrolls III: Morrowind*, though it is present to an extent. We must take each game and type of game on its own terms.

If I had continued (and I am sure most of you would have deserted me), we would have converged on a "feature system" with which to categorize game play and the pleasures connected to it. Many games would not have been "pure" examples, but, rather, mixtures of features more saliently present in purer cases. Here, by the way, purity is not better than impurity. We have to take each on its own terms. Such a feature system, while a structuralist's dream—and certainly the sort of dream I dreamed when I formerly practiced linguistics straight—is not my dream here. My dream here is just to celebrate the potential of good video games, the technologies by which they are made, the intelligence by which they are designed and played, and the pleasures that are part and parcel of that intelligence.

When I was a student, now many years ago, one of the things I studied was logic. One type of logic of some relevance to philosophy dealt with "possible worlds". In this type of logic one asked whether a sentence was true or false, or an argument valid or invalid, not just in the real world, but in all possible worlds, all the worlds that the human mind could imagine. Sentences that are true in all possible worlds turn out, of course, to be trivial, things like "Circles are round". Sentences that are false in all possible worlds are equally obvious, things like "Circles are square". The only interesting sentences are those that are true in some possible worlds and not others, things like "Cancer does not exist" This is, of course, not true in our real world, but we can imagine a world in which it is.

It is an interesting exercise to imagine a possible, but not real world in which something is true that we would hope and wish were true in the real world. When you do this, however, you have to imagine all the other things that would have to hold in that world—all the other things that would have to differ from the real world—if the cherished truth was to hold, as well. What would a world have to look like if no child was to go to bed hungry or face abuse from powerful adults? If the economy was to flourish without destroying the environment? If people made peace with the creativity with which they make war? Perhaps such worlds can't ever exist 100%—but, then, we don't really know until we imagine them and then try—and, then, too, being 80% there is better than 50% and surely better than 0.

Video games are worlds, whether these be *Tetris* or *Morrowind*. Their designers are world imaginers and world builders. Their players co-author these worlds in the act of playing them. If they use the tools every more readily available to them, they can also modify games in ways that let them share at yet higher levels in the act of designing.

My nine-year-old uses the a scenario editor that comes with *Age of Mythology* to build his own environments, stock them with characters, and set loose various forms of interaction. He also reads about mythology in books and on websites, writes about it, watches films and goes to exhibits about it. He shares this interest in talk, play, and reading with his friends. It opens up worlds in which to explore values, themes, and emotions of great import, to imagine why things are as they are, how they might have been, and what they could be.

Play with worlds, building worlds, relating these worlds to other worlds across various media: video games are part of the heart of this matter. They are worlds in a box. I have argued that they feed the soul's desire for agency, control, and meaningfulness. I have argued they hold out new paths for deeper learning. But what I love about them is that they hold out the promise of imagining new worlds and setting sparks loose that may make people want to make these worlds real.

That promise has barely been explored. We are just at the beginning. Games are soothing torn souls. They are reuniting pleasure and learning. But in the future they will, I hope, allow us to take off for new real worlds right here on earth, worlds that are better for all our souls. But we will have to be careful not to let games be co-opted by our old cultures and lesser selves. There is more than money at stake here. Our souls are at stake.

REFERENCES

Aarseth, E. J. (1998). Cybertext: Perspectives in ergotic literature. Baltimore, MD: Johns Hopkins University Press.

Barsalou, L. W. (1999a). Language comprehension: Archival memory or preparation for situated action. Discourse Processes 28: 61-80.

Barsalou, L. W. (1999b). Perceptual symbol systems. Behavioral and Brain Sciences 22: 577-660.

Bauman, Z. (2000). Individualized society. Cambridge: Polity Press.

Beck. U. (1992). Risk society. London: Sage.

Bereiter, C. & Scardamalia, M. (1993). Surpassing ourselves: An inquiry into the nature and implications of expertise. Chicago: Open Court.

Blum, D. (2002). Love at Goon Park: Harry Harlow and the science of affection. New York: Perseus.

Clark, A. (1993). Associative engines: Connectionism, concepts, and representational change. Cambridge: Cambridge University Press.

Damasio, A. R. (1995). Descartes' error: Emotion, reason, and the human brain. New York: Quill.

Damasio, A. R. (2003). Looking for Spinoza: Joy, sorrow, and the feeling brain. New York: Harvest Books.

Dickinson, E. (1924). The complete poems. Boston: Little, Brown.

diSessa, A. A. (2000). Changing minds: Computers, learning, and literacy. Cambridge, Mass.: MIT Press.

Gee, J. P. (1992). The social mind. New York: Bergin & Garvey.

Gee, J. P. (2003). What video games have to teach us about learning and literacy. New York: Palgrave/Macmillan.

Gee, J. P. (2004). Situated language and learning: A critique of traditional schooling. London: Routledge.

Gee, J. P., Hull, G., & Lankshear, C. (1996). The new work order: Behind the language of the new capitalism. Boulder, CO: Westview Press.

Giddens, A. (1991). Modernity and self-identity. Cambridge: Polity Press.

Giddens, A. (1992). The transformation of intimacy. Cambridge: Polity Press.

Glenberg, A. M. (1997). What is memory for. Behavioral and Brain Sciences 20: 1-55.

Glenberg, A. M. & Robertson, D. A. (1999). Indexical understanding of instructions. Discourse Processes 28: 1-26.

Greenfield, P. (1984). Media and the mind of the child: From print to television, video games and computers. Cambridge, Mass.: Harvard University Press.

Greider, W. (1997). One world, ready or not: The manic logic of global capitalism. New York: Simon & Schuster.

Holland, J. H. (1999). Emergence: From chaos to order. New York: Perseus.

Hutchins, E. (1995). Cognition in the Wild. Cambridge, MA: MIT Press.

Juul, J. (2004). Half-Real: Video games between real rules and fictional worlds. Doctoral dissertation, University of Copenhagen.

Kantor, N. F. (2004). The last knight: The twilight of the Middle Ages and the birth of the Modern Era. New York: Free Press.

Kauffman, S. (1995). At home in the universe: The search for laws of self-organization and complexity. Oxford: Oxford University Press.

Kent, S. L. (2001). The ultimate history of video games: The story behind the craze that touched our lives and changed the world. Roseville, Calif.: Prima.

Kelly, K. (1994). Out of control: The new biology of machines, social systems, and the economic world. Reading, Mass.: Addison-Wesley.

King, L., Ed. (2002). Game on: The history and culture of videogames. New York: Universe Publishing.

King, B. & Borland, J. (2003). Dungeons and dreamers: The rise of computer game culture from geek to chic. New York: McGraw-Hill.

Lam, W. S. E. (2000). L2 literacy and the design of the self: A case study of a teenager writing on the Internet. TESOL Quarterly 34: 457-482.

Laurel, B. (1991). Computers as theatre. Reading, MA: Addison-Wesley.

Margolis. H. (1987). Patterns, thinking, and cognition: A theory of judgment. Chicago: University of Chicago Press.

Matthews, M. R. (1994). Science teaching: The role of history and philosophy of science.

Murray, J. H. (1997). Hamlet on the holodeck: The future of narrative in cyberspace. New York: Free Press.

Ochs, E., Gonzales, P., & Jacoby, S. (1996). "When I come down I'm in the domain state". In E. Ochs, E. Schegloff, & S. A. Thompson, Eds., Interaction and Grammar. Cambridge: Cambridge University Press, pp. 328-369.

Poole. S. (2000). Trigger happy: Videogames and the entertainment revolution. New York: Arcade.

Reich, R. B. (1992). The work of nations. New York: Vintage.

Rifkin, J. (2000). The age of access: The new culture of hypercapitalism where all of life is a paid-for experience. New York: Jeremy P. Tarcher/Putnam.

Salin, K. & Zimmerman, E. (2003). Rules of play: Game design fundamentals. Cambridge, MA: MIT Press.

Shaffer, D. W. (2004). Pedagogical praxis: The professions as models for post-industrial education. Teachers College Record 10: 1401-1421.

Shermer, M. (1997). Why people believe weird things. New York: W. H. Freeman.

Taylor, C. (1992). The ethics of authenticity. Cambridge, MA: Harvard University Press.

Taylor, C. (1994). The politics of recognition. In Taylor, C., Appiah, K. A., Rockefeller, S.C., Waltzer, M., & Wolf, S. (1994). Multiculturalism: Examining the politics of recognition. Ed. by A. Gutman. Princeton: Princeton University Press, pp. 25-73.

Waldrip-Fruin, N. & Harrigan, P. (2004). First person: New Media as story, performance, and game. Cambridge, MA: MIT Press.

Wolf. M. J. P. (2002). The medium of the video game. Austin, TX: University of Texas Press.

Wolf, M. J. P. & Perron, B. (2003). The video game theory reader. London: Routledge.